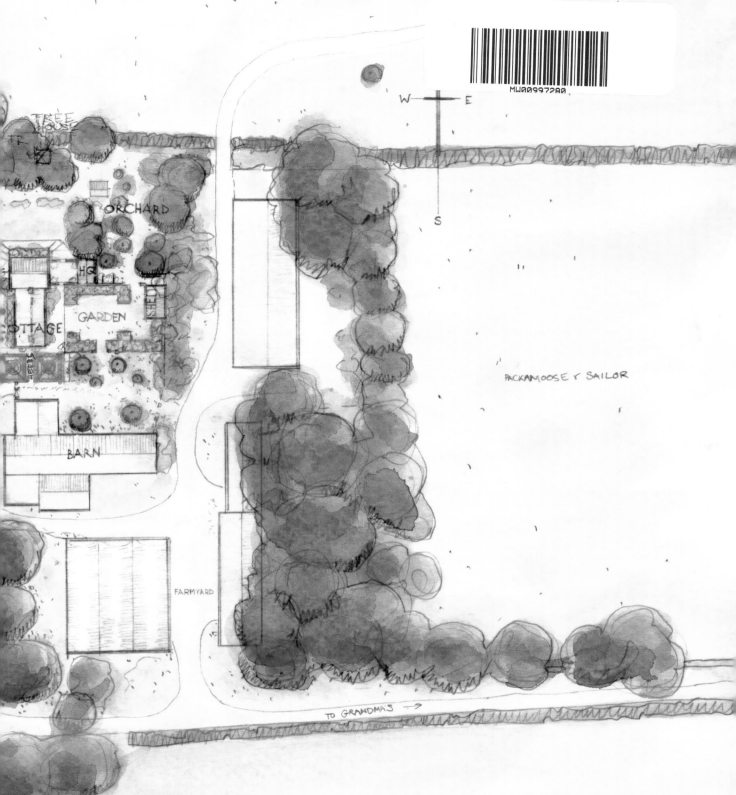

TREE
HOUSE

ORCHARD

HQ

SHED

GARDEN

COTTAGE

BARN

FARMYARD

W   E

S

PACKAMOOSE & SAILOR

TO GRANDMA'S →

REEN FARM, GARDEN PLAN   M B

blue
rider
press

FARM FROM HOME

Also by Amanda Brooks

I Love Your Style
Always Pack a Party Dress

*To my beloved daddy, Stephen Cutter (1940–2016),
who gave me my first taste of farm life*

FARM FROM HOME

A Year of Stories, Pictures, and Recipes from a City Girl in the Country

AMANDA BROOKS

WITH PHOTOGRAPHS BY THE AUTHOR

BLUE RIDER PRESS

NEW YORK

blue
rider
press

An imprint of Penguin Random House LLC
375 Hudson Street
New York, New York 10014

"In Praise of Country Life," published by Frederick Muller Ltd, 1949. Edited by Alison Uttley, p. 42.

ISBN 9781101983447 (hardcover)
ISBN 9781101983461 (ebook)

Printed in China
1 3 5 7 9 10 8 6 4 2

RICHARD PANDISCIO, CREATIVE DIRECTOR
WILLIAM LOCCISANO, DESIGNER
ENDPAPERS BY MIRANDA BROOKS

Let the wealthy and great roll in splendor and state
I envy them not, I declare it
I eat my own lamb, my own chickens and ham
I shear my own fleece and I wear it
I have lawns, I have bowers
I have fruits, I have flowers
The lark is my morning alarmer
So jolly boys now, here's God speed the plough
Long life and success to the farmer

"God Speed the Plough," author unknown, nineteenth century

CONTENTS

RECIPES

INTRODUCTION

JUNE 20, 2012, United Airlines flight 8, from Newark to Heathrow. That is how we arrived to live in England for our "yearlong creative sabbatical," the one that isn't yet over. The four of us, well, actually five of us—myself; my husband, Christopher; our nearly eleven-year-old daughter, Coco; our eight-year-old son, Zach; and our beloved three-year-old rescue dog, Ginger—all boarded the plane that day feeling completely and utterly exhausted. The last twenty-four hours in New York City had been never-ending. You know that feeling when every bone in your body is telling you to stop what you are doing and lie down to get some sleep, and you aren't even close to being finished? That's how it was. We packed, made lists, copied keys, labeled the dog crate, and cleaned out closets right until the very last minute. I even made an eleventh-hour dash to my doctor when I broke out in a terribly itchy rash on my back that turned out to be shingles. Yes, from the stress. And that was all before we had to say our final, tearful good-byes to my mother, a few of our closest friends, and the children's nanny, Pam, who had been with us since Coco was just a year old.

For a moment, we considered taking the *Queen Mary 2* across the Atlantic for our arrival in England. It seemed like an inspired way to decompress from our relocating frenzy and endless emotional farewells, and we loved the idea of arriving for our new life in such romantic style. But my excitement was quickly extinguished when I learned we'd have to wear black tie for dinner every night on the ship. After twenty years of dressing to the nines each day for work in the fashion industry, the thought of having to be formal for each night of the seven-day ocean passage, especially while surrounded by a bunch of cruise-ship enthusiasts, was the nail in the coffin of that idea.

The biggest concern about the eventual plane journey was Ginger and her fragile disposition. Given her rescue dog vulnerability and her melodramatic reactions to thunderstorms (spread-eagle, lying on top of me, shaking all over), I was worried that the loud noises and the uneven movements of the plane might just be too much for her. We followed the airline instructions to the letter and read

Looking into our cottage garden past the rosa mundi rosebush, a giant belle etoile philadelphus,
and some cow parsley. Philadelphus, which flowers in June, is my favorite flower to cut for the house;
it has the most delicious smell—kind of like bubblegum, but in a good way.

Three days after we moved to England, Ginger followed Coco down to her riding lesson a few fields away from our house. Polo surprised us all when he came right up and gave Gingy a cuddle as she sat on the bench. I don't think Gingy knew what to do with that kind of attention from a horse.

every possible Web site with pointers and tips for dogs flying in cargo. Then, to add to the worrying, we called Heathrow the day before the flight to clear Ginger for customs and were told that the wait to pick her up after the flight would be five hours! After begging and pleading with the airline staff to have her expedited, they casually mentioned we could have her delivered directly to our house an hour and a half away in Oxfordshire for a mere eighty-eight pounds (about a hundred and forty dollars). While we quickly jumped at that option, it only prolonged the time until we would know that Ginger was okay. During the flight, every sound, jolt, and awkward motion of the plane had me worried about our precious baby down below. Nevertheless, at three p.m. on that Thursday afternoon, a few hours after we arrived at our cottage on the farm where Christopher grew up and where we would now live, a minivan pulled up and we all ran outside with great anticipation. We opened the crate with anxious hands, and Ginger jumped right out, doing her signature wiggle dance, in which her unusually long and fluffy tail shakes so wildly that it swings her entire body from side to side.

The next task was to introduce Ginger to the animals. Our cottage is right in the middle of a farmyard, and at that time the stables right beside us contained horses, donkeys, and pigs. Given that Ginger was terrified of the two Great Danes that lived in our New York City neighborhood, I didn't have high hopes for her reaction to much stranger and larger animals. To our surprise, however, she briefly cowered in front of the pigs, didn't seem at all fazed by the donkeys, and ran up dangerously close to the horses, who were being saddled up for a ride. Coco mounted one and took off. It had long been a dream of hers that Ginger would follow as she rode her pony, Polo, around the farm, but Ginger stayed right by my side, not budging. "Give her some time," I suggested. And when Coco eased Polo into a trot as they were nearing the woods, Ginger took off after her and followed them until they all reappeared together an hour later. Ginger was wet, muddy, and out of breath, but I have never seen her happier.

The timing of our late-June move to the farm was planned for various reasons. We wanted to arrive in summer, perhaps the most optimistic time of the year and also the season most familiar to us (we had spent many Junes and Julys at the farm in the past). We wanted to give ourselves a few months to settle in before the kids started at their new school, and we wanted plenty of time for American friends to visit us at the farm and help the kids realize that they would still be very much a part of our lives. We promised ourselves a week of solid unpacking and chore-doing, and then we would surrender to the ongoing new-life chaos enough to enjoy ourselves, our family, and our friends, and make sure to connect with all the wonderful reasons why we had chosen to live here.

And that's how it started. Our one-year break from New York that has now lasted six and become—dare I say it?—permanent. I don't know if I would have had the nerve to leave New York City if I told myself it would be forever, or at least for a good long while. But regardless of what it took to convince myself to get on that plane, once we got here and made a dent in the herculean task of settling into our new rural lives in another country, on another continent no less, it became apparent that we weren't going anywhere anytime soon. So here we are, feeling good about our decision, still marveling at how our kids (and ourselves) are thriving, and settled into the idea of staying put for the time being.

Coco taking Polo for a hack (English-speak for a ride) around the farm.

People ask me all the time if my English country life is really as good as it looks on Instagram. As a highly visual person who majored in photography in college and then worked in fashion for twenty years, I am a self-admitted aesthetic perfectionist. In fact, my kids call my obsession with order, discipline, and every detail in our surroundings my "attention surplus disorder." So I can see why people wonder whether my life can possibly be as idyllic, romantic, and peaceful as it looks in the photographs I create and choose to share. They are right to question it, because the answer of course is that no life can be that good, that tidy, that immaculately balanced! Those are just my photographs.

But I also believe that people asking me that question are really wanting to know: *Is a life like that actually attainable? If I left my stressful city job and moved to the countryside in order to live a quieter, more meaningful life for myself and for my family, would it really be possible to actually be . . . happy?* Before moving to England and simultaneously discovering the miracle of Instagram, I wasn't aware of how many people had the same inclination that I had had, whether it was to simplify their responsibilities, to live a more peaceful life, or to make it easier to focus on family or animals or nature. And then once I acted on that notion, it was as though I had become the guinea pig, the subject of the experiment. *How is it?* everyone wanted to know.

I had wondered the exact same thing a few years before when I read an article in *Vogue* about model Stella Tennant's rural life. Stella, her husband, and their four children had upped sticks from New York and moved to a dreamy farmhouse in the Scottish Borders. I loved reading about the balance she had created between her wholesome country life and her occasional city life, flying to New York for the Met Ball or to Paris to appear in the next Chanel ad campaign. That story planted a seed in my head that grew closer to reality when I ran into Stella at a party in New York just before I accepted the job of fashion director at Barneys. I had all the same questions my Instagram followers had. *Did she love it? Was it as great as it looked? Did she have friends? Was it ever lonely? Did she feel as though the rest of the world had forgotten about her? Were she and her husband both equally happy there?* Her truthful yet mostly encouraging answers to those questions stayed with me and swirled around in my head right until I made my own decision to make a similar move.

This book is an attempt to answer the question of what life is like for me on our farm, to tell you more about the range of my experience and my family's, beyond my idealized photographs. My writing and my day-to-day life are much messier than the pictures I take, and so I want you to see that other side. What is it like for

*Christopher is particular about cultivating his compost. He has it on a three-year cycle
in three different bays, each one in a different phase of decomposition.*

a city girl who suddenly, albeit by choice, finds herself smack in the middle of the countryside? For an outspoken, direct, and possibly even precocious American who is now surrounded by self-deprecating, reserved, and far more intellectual English country folk? During my last ten years in New York, I was defined as a creative director, a business owner, and then a fashion director. So how does it feel now to be defined—by myself and others—primarily as a wife and mother, and occasionally as a part-time writer/consultant?

The short answer, for now, is that I am happier on a much deeper and more mature level than I was in New York. My priorities are straight-ish; my everyday is filled with quality people, quality time, and quality activities. But there has also been a very long process of letting go that is still sometimes painful. Occasionally I find myself wanting the best of both worlds—city and country—and that is often not as attainable as I might want it to be. I often have a fear of becoming too comfortable and feel unsure about how I will continue on a fulfilling career path from our farm. I love working, and sometimes I look at my fifty-nine-year-old husband and worry that he is, in fact, retired. Yes, he manages his existing real estate business in New York via telephone and e-mail and the occasional work trip, but he largely spends his time in his other capacity as an artist, or gardening, riding, and managing the farm. Sometimes I say to him, "Are you retired? Is that what this life is?" He just laughs and avoids a direct answer. But I know that I am certainly not retired. I have decades of working years left and have not even come close to accomplishing all that I have planned.

I get hundreds of other questions too: *Do you miss fashion? Do you miss New York City? How do you cope with the weather? With the darkness? Do you have a routine? What do you wear on the farm? How do you get food? Do you have to cook every meal? Are there any restaurants that deliver to the farm?*

I'll give you one answer up front: yes, there is a restaurant that delivers to the farm. Just *one*. It's a fantastic Indian restaurant in Chipping Norton called Café Le Raj. The first, second, and third time they brought us our order, it took them more than an hour to find our cottage, so finally they told me that the next time I called, to just announce myself as "the American lady on the farm," and they would know where to bring the food. We are such good and loyal customers that when I call now and say, "It's the American lady," the waiters all start to cheer and the manager takes over to make sure we are well served and the food is delivered efficiently. You can take the girl out of New York City . . .

Speaking of life in New York, since leaving I have recognized that the need for money there is endless. Enough is simply never enough. Skyrocketing school fees, a nanny, a housekeeper, kids' extracurricular activities, meals out, taxis, Metro cards, groceries, clothing, doctor's appointments, apartment décor, mortgage payments, maintenance fees—all suck up your income nearly as soon as it lands in your bank account. During the twenty years I lived there, I never felt that I made enough money. And there were a few years where I made *a lot* of money.

On the farm, we have all those same family expenses but fewer of the lifestyle ones. We cook at home much more than we eat out, we live quite far away from tempting shops, the English health care system is more affordable, and the general sense of well-being and happiness distracts from the need for retail therapy.

All this to say that I personally live off far less money than I did in New York. I have a set monthly budget made up of book writing payments, some of the rental income from our New York apartment, and the occasional consulting job. It's enough money to live on and affords me the luxury of being home when the kids are out of school and having time in my daily life to walk the dogs, ride a horse, and cook the majority of meals at home. When the offer of a new consulting job comes in, especially if it's a lucrative one, I now have the flexibility to ask myself if it's really how I want to spend my time. Sometimes the answer is yes, and other times it's a firm no. In New York, I didn't feel I could ever afford to turn down opportunities to increase my bottom line, especially when I had employees working for me. With the new sense of freedom I have created for myself on the farm, I often end up negotiating better deals for myself because I am willing to walk away if it's

Harvested vegetables from the Fairgreen kitchen garden.

not exactly what I want. I know it sounds like a huge cliché, but despite the more modest lifestyle, my life has never felt richer or more fulfilling.

I know people are wondering, how *do* I spend my time in the country? When I wrote my first book, *I Love Your Style*, in 2009, I wrote it in between handling half a dozen major brands that were clients of my fashion consulting company. Now, writing is the vast majority of what I do and yet it seems to take me much longer to churn out a book, so what am I doing the rest of the time? I wondered that for a while too. When we first moved here, I asked Christopher what people in the countryside do now that farming is largely outsourced. "You'll see," he said, "'living in the country' is a job title within itself." With most country folk or farm owners no longer having the resources to hire lots of household help, or any at all in some cases, it takes time to make food, tend your garden, look after your animals, and also to enjoy it—to share a meal with friends, go for walks, ride your horses. We do employ a few people who help us run our farm, but not so many that they are turning our apples into juice, our rhubarb into crumble, or walking our dogs within their paid hours.

My mother-in-law's friend Harry Westropp hunting in Leicestershire in the 1970s. I never grow tired of looking at traditional British hunting attire.

So what am I making, cooking, doing on the farm? And what am I *not* doing? Having tried nearly every country pastime, from knitting to riding ("on a horse" is implicit in England; no one here refers to it as "horse riding"—or worse, "horseback riding"—as we do in America) and from gardening to cooking in my first year here, what has stuck, and what have I delegated or just given up on altogether?

One of the things I love most unequivocally about country life is how connected I feel to the seasons. Having spent so much time in nature, I have come to realize that instead of the four typical seasons we all know, there are actually twelve here in England, one for every month in the calendar.

My life here is inevitably and intrinsically dictated by what is going on outside: Is it too muddy to ride? Is it so cold that I have to start my workday by making a fire in my office's wood-burning stove? Is the unexpected sunshine summoning me to do some weeding in the garden? Do I need to defrost food for dinner, or is there something fresh I can use from the garden? So I will tell you about a year, my year, in the country. But it's not just about one year; it's about what I have learned and the experience I have gained in the six years I have lived here, from month to month.

I am not an expert on English country life, just an enthusiast. The inspiration I draw from where I live now is stronger than anywhere else I have ever called home. After twenty years in fashion trying out every trend imaginable, I felt like a chameleon in my New York life. My English life, in contrast, has helped me to embrace my own roots and traditions from home and combine them with new inspiration in a way that has helped me finally define who I am. My appreciation of faded floral wallpaper, the clothes that people wear for riding, the way fruit is so diligently preserved for the winter months, the impeccable manners with which people treat one another, the appreciation of culture, the deep connection to nature—and the unwillingness to get rid of anything at all—led me to become a huge fan of England and its way of life, and I hope you will be too, after reading this book.

Many people encouraged me to write about my country life when I first moved here in 2012. It was tempting, but I was too close to the new experience to have anything very useful to say about it. Plus, I wanted a year just to live the dream. And I did. I experienced every single country cliché you could imagine, from learning to make jam to reading Jilly Cooper novels. But now that it's been a few more years, I have returned to a more realistic approach to life and started to ask myself what my future looks like. Can I continue my career from here? Or am I just getting more and more used to the notion of living a "country life"? My kids will possibly (hopefully) go to college in America and then Christopher and I would likely spend more time in New York again—but would we ever get back on the treadmill of ambition and success? For now, that is still a ways off, enough so to represent the future. And so my future is here for now, and this is how I am working toward it.

My bedroom. The Laura Ashley floral wallpaper has been there since the '80s when the cottage was first converted from a cart shed into a home.

How the Farm Works

Christopher and the kids and I live in a cottage that is in the middle of a farm-yard containing 1820s limestone barns and stables, 1930s corrugated-steel Dutch barns, 1960s hangar-style concrete cattle sheds and workshops, and the old pig-geries, which are now a painting studio for Christopher and a small guesthouse. Our farmyard is pretty much smack in the middle of a larger seven-hundred-acre farm that has belonged to Christopher's family since the 1940s. While we all call it "the farm," it is actually made up of two farms that share a border and function pretty much as a whole. Acreage is all relative in England—some of our friends have large, multi-thousand-acre estates, while others live in the middle of a vil-lage with a small garden. But on the whole, where we live is more rural and spread out than anything you would find within a two-hour radius of, say, New York or Los Angeles. I wouldn't want to be anywhere, in any circumstance, other than exactly where we are.

I took this picture of the cottage in 1997, the first time I visited Fairgreen Farm.
Amazing to see how young the espaliered pear trees on the side of the house still were then.

A bird's-eye view of our cottage and farmyard from the "owl's nest" in our treehouse.

The location and position of our house and surrounding farm are as picturesque as the most charming Cotswolds images your mind, or any online search engine, can conjure up. It's also immensely private and quiet. Other neighboring farms are visible in the far distance, but from our cottage, I am not able to see any buildings other than the ones on the farm. At night, there are no cities twinkling in the distance, only stars and occasionally the moon. From my bedroom window, the only human-created light I can see when I go to bed is the one coming from my mother-in-law Caroline's bedroom across the fields, which I find immensely comforting when my husband is away for the night. Sometimes I stand at the window and recall that my mother-in-law lived here for more than twenty years all by herself, her husband having died long ago and her children off exploring the world. Even though there is nothing at all menacing about the farm—in fact, it's the only countryside where I'm not afraid to go outside in the dark—I still can't imagine living on such a big piece of land all by myself. These days, my mother-in-law's entire immediate family lives on the farm, and she tells us often how lucky she feels and how much pleasure it gives her to be surrounded by all her three children and six grandchildren.

Fairgreen Farm. That's good old Mr. Teddy in the field with the sheep. Sadly he is long gone now.

Christopher's hand-painted sign directing traffic to our farmyard and to his sister's house.
People often confuse the two, as they share the same name.

On the west side is Fairgreen Farm—that's our farm. There is a big house called Fairgreen House, where Christopher's grandparents used to live. Christopher's older sister lives there now with her family. In dividing up the property so that everybody got their fair share, she got the big house and Christopher got the farmyard and much of the land. Just up the hill and adjacent to us is Castle Barn Farm, where Christopher's mother lives in a cottage and where Christopher's brother and his family live in a converted barn and stables. With siblings and parents and cousins all living on one piece of land, we are often referred to jokingly as "the Brooks commune," or "The Reservation," for having lived here for so long. Many of our neighbors have extra cottages and outbuildings that they rent out to friends or family, but we are the only family that has every immediate member (plus in-laws!) all living on one property. This setup is not without its occasional drama, but there is strength in numbers, and we all love one another. Holidays are epic: if everyone is in attendance and we add in extended family and a few friends, we often total more than thirty people at one table.

Our entire farm (the two joined together) was once a satellite farm for Sarsden, a grand seventeenth-century stately home and estate next door. Large estates often used the farmland immediately surrounding the house (known traditionally as the Home Farm) for their own personal purposes and supplies—gardens, planted fruit and vegetables, and of course livestock to eat. Our land, which starts about a half mile from the main house, was likely run by tenant farmers even in its heyday, with income going to the landowner as a subsidy. Fairgreen House would have belonged to the head farmer and his family. As farming became less lucrative and land and hereditary taxes increased, many families sold off portions of their land. In 1922, the Sarsden estate was reduced from five thousand acres down to four hundred, creating the opportunity for Christopher's grandfather, Noel Brand Brooks, to buy Fairgreen and Castle Barn Farms after the Second World War. Reminders of the estate's history are still present on and around the farm. Two sets of imposing stone pillars that mark the original entrance to Sarsden remain at the borders of our farm. There is also Lord Moreton's Seat, a lovely stone bench marking the favorite spot from which the onetime Sarsden owner could sit and look out over all his land, which sits just adjacent to our gallops (where the racehorses train). It's a lovely place to let the dogs run free or to watch the sun set.

Fairgreen House when it was lived in by Christopher's grandparents, starting in the 1940s.

The pillars between Fairgreen and the neighboring farm. They used to represent the entrance to Sarsden, a stately home to which Fairgreen Farm once belonged.

*Christopher's grandfather Noel Brand Brooks, who
bought all of Fairgreen Farm and Castle Barn Farm
in the 1940s, picks apples in the Fairgreen kitchen
garden with Charlie, Christopher's younger brother.*

Historically, the Cotswolds were part of the medieval wool trade. In the fifteenth century, this was the equivalent of the oil business in that the whole world depended on this product—wool—and there were no synthetic alternatives. Wool production comprised a dynamic triangular trading partnership among England, France, and Belgium: the English produced the wool, the French wove it, and the Belgians dyed it. Because the soil of the Cotswolds is brash (a lightweight mixture of limestone and soil that is very free-draining, or porous), it was possible for animals to graze this land year-round. The great medieval churches for which the region is known were all built on the back of this industry. During the Second World War, however, the government dictated that this land be put under the plow to produce crops so that England didn't have to rely on other countries for food sources. What this meant was a much less pastoral approach to farming in the drive for efficiency. For our farm, this brought the phasing out of all the horse teams that pulled plows and any other manual job that required literal horsepower.

Christopher's grandfather Noel Brooks was a businessman who had previously run a large and successful coal mine in the north of England. In 1946, he and his wife bought Fairgreen and Castle Barn Farms in order to live a quieter life after the coal-mining business had faltered. In farming, there were so many unexpected variables—such as a big rain before a hay harvest, the trial and error of growing new crops, and understanding the right kind of trees to plant—to which his temperament was not particularly suited and his experience was limited. Noel introduced the farm's first tractors shortly after acquiring the farm in the late 1940s but found that they struggled to pull the plows through the brashy soil. After a few false starts, they eventually found the right machinery to manage the land. Sadly, this new strategy of farming in England also led to the removal of more than two million miles of medieval hedgerows throughout the countryside that had been laid for livestock over centuries.

During this time, it was still possible to make a living from farming by combining resources and products. At Fairgreen and Castle Barn, there was livestock—mostly sheep, due to the fact that the existing stone walls were highly effective in containing them, but also some shorthorn dairy cattle and about two hundred pigs. They also relied heavily on the growth and sale of cereals such as wheat, barley, and oats. In the 1960s, when Christopher's father, Robert, became involved in managing the farm, there were all the usual tensions between father and son about how things should be done, but after a while, Noel found relief in handing over the reins to Bob, who took a more practical and informed approach to farming having grown up on the farm and attended the Royal Agricultural College (now the Royal Agricultural University) in Cirencester. He built modern grain dryers and grain handling machinery and installed cattle sheds. During this time, there were eight full-time workers on the farm.

Robert Noel Brand Brooks, Christopher's father, on the farm in the 1970s.

Castle Barn in the 1960s, the house where Christopher grew up and where his mother still lives.

Then in the 1970s, there was a major shift when the UK decided to join the EU. Farming policy went from being a national policy to a European federal one. The EU plan was to set a minimum price for all farm goods. From that point onward, people farmed what seemed to be the most lucrative product, which in a lot of cases wasn't the product best suited for their land. Consequently, for our farm, it meant the end of commercial livestock (primarily pigs, sheep, and cattle).

Herman the German

Rickyard Cottage, where we live, has an interesting history in relation to the war. In 1944, a man called Herman Seidel (later nicknamed Herman the German) was wounded at Stalingrad and on one of the last medical trains to get out before German general Friedrich Paulus's Sixth Army got cut off in what was to be a turning point of the Second World War. Herman never saw anyone in his regiment ever again. He was sent on guard duty to Biarritz, France, in order to recuperate, but when D-day happened, he was drafted into the Normandy defenses. One afternoon, he was riding on the outside of a tank down a highway when over the brow of a hill in another direction came an American tank. The driver of his tank turned hard right straight through a farmhouse, bringing the roof down on all the people clinging to the outside of the tank. Herman's leg was pinched badly. He dragged himself into a shell hole and waited. Eventually Herman was captured by the Americans in France and shipped off to a prisoner-of-war camp in England. Once he was fit enough, he joined the other German prisoners who were sent out to work on the land at various farms during the day and were taken back to the POW camp and locked up at night. Herman was assigned to work at Fairgreen Farm. When it became clear that Germany was going to lose the war, the Brookses were permitted to house Herman on the farm, as long as he was locked in at night. For many years he slept in the hayloft of our cottage (then a rickyard shed, thus the name), which is now my bedroom! At the conclusion of the war, when Herman learned that the part of Germany he was raised in had fallen into Russian hands, he had no will to return home. Herman eventually married a local English girl, Barbara, the blacksmith's daughter, and they raised two children in one of the cottages on the edge of the farm where Barbara still lives to this day. Herman lived and worked at Fairgreen, eventually becoming the foreman of the farm, until he died in the mid-1980s.

With increasing efficiency throughout the decades since the war, it has become harder and harder for small farms such as ours to be viable. For example, a modern combine harvester costs three hundred thousand dollars! So how do we use our land now that farming is an increasingly challenging way to produce income? We do still farm the arable land (that which is able to be plowed); we no longer farm it ourselves, however. Christopher's father died relatively young, at age forty-eight in the late 1970s, and since then, Christopher's mother has run the farm in partnership with professional local farmers: pooling resources and sharing equipment reaps the benefits of scale. In recent years, mechanization means that people weren't replaced when they retired, reducing the number of people required to keep the farm going.

Christopher standing in the limestone quarry he created on our farm, 1997. It's his Howard Roark moment.

In addition to traditional agricultural farming, we have a limestone quarry that contributes to the income of the farm. About thirty-five years ago, Christopher did an apprenticeship in architectural masonry. During that time, it occurred to him that he could perhaps reopen an old quarry he knew had once existed on the farm. He went down to the quarry one day and pulled out some large pieces of limestone that proved to be viable as building materials. With that result, he partnered with a local builder and started a company for harvesting, cutting, and installing limestone locally. Stone from our farm has been used to build floors, walls, terraces, and entire houses in most of the surrounding villages and towns. By now we have pretty much cleaned out one whole band of stone on one side of the driveway, and we're now making a big dent across on the other side.

And finally, in the fields around our house we have horses. Most of them are for pleasure—hacking, Pony Club, and hunting, mostly. But from time to time we also have a couple of young racehorses— belonging to my brother-in-law and mother-in-law, who partner in breeding them—just eating and growing until they are big enough to train and race and eventually sell for a profit.

Sylvie, mare, 16.3hh (the horse's height). Christopher's hunter. She's a badass.

PackerMoose (aka Moose), filly, 16.1hh (at age three). She was born and bred on the farm. She'll either be a hunter or an eventer.

Polo (aka Po), gelding, 14.2hh. My boy. Both Coco and my niece rode Po before I did. He taught me everything I know about hunting.

Cushtie (aka Cush), mare, 14.3hh. The pony of a friend who spends school holidays and summers with us.

Tottie (aka Tots), mare, 16.3hh. Coco's eventing horse. She's a pain to handle but is an amazing jumper. She and Coco won their very first One Day Event together.

Jake (aka Jakey Boy), gelding, 15.1hh. Coco's hunter. He's a bit small for her now, but he is amazing out hunting. He jumps everything in sight.

Petra and Shalom (aka Sha), mares, both 16.1hh. Petra doesn't belong to us anymore, but Shalom does. She used to be my horse, but I don't like hunting her, so she serves as an extra horse on the farm for houseguests or when another horse is injured.

Chip, (aka Chippie Darling), gelding, 10.2hh. He belongs to family friends who visit the farm on holidays.

Megan, mare, 17hh. My brother-in-law's hunter, seen here with her foal PackerMoose. Megan once won the Heythrop gate-jumping competition, jumping more than six feet!

Sailor (aka SaiSai), gelding, 13.2hh. Our beloved boy. He's well into his thirties, and nearly every child on and around the farm has spent time on Sailor. When Coco took him to Pony Club camp, he won Most-Willing Pony three years in a row.

Richard (left) and Sinead (right) bringing in the horses to be shod (receive new shoes).

Because farming today in general requires far fewer workers, many vacancies were left in local farm and estate cottages that would have traditionally housed them. This available real estate created opportunities for weekenders from London to rent cottages on lovely old estates and eventually drove up the price of local real estate. Cottages on our farm that would once have been deemed of very little value now bring in good income, and with the influx of more sophisticated locals, pubs, farmshops, and even schools have improved dramatically, making it a more comfortable place for city girls like me to call home on a full-time basis.

And how do we look after the farm? It's pretty much a skeleton crew compared to the good old days. First and foremost, there is Richard, who has worked on the farm for forty-seven years. He started off as a laborer in his twenties and has been the head dog of the farm ever since Christopher's father died in 1976. Richard is semiretired these days, but he is still around six days a week, starting at seven a.m. Christopher's brother and sister both employ a gardener, but we don't, as Christopher prefers to tend to our garden himself, with the occasional planting or weeding help from me.

We have a groom, Sinead, who works a few hours each day looking after our horses, who typically range in quantity from six to ten. She is incredibly knowledgeable, having worked for many years on a racing yard, and she does everything from feeding them to treating injuries, maintaining the tack to ensuring they are fit for us to hunt, compete, or just simply to take out for a canter around the fields. Additionally, Sinead helps out with caring for our two pigs and our pet lamb, Juice, by giving them hard feed in winter when there isn't enough fresh grass to fill their bellies and keep them healthy.

Then there is Tomak. As no one had properly lived in our farmyard for twenty years and there are many buildings abandoned by the reduced farming, Christopher and I employ a Polish builder who does all our maintenance and renovation work. Tomak lives in one of the converted stables and is the only other person who lives in the farmyard with us. Although we keep a respectful distance during our downtime, Tomak has lived here for almost five years and pretty much feels like family to us. The presence of a big, strong man close by gives me a reassuring feeling of security when Christopher is away or in case of any emergencies.

Tomak (left) and Christopher (right) planting oak saplings in middle Fairgreen field.

Since we moved to England (or, in Christopher's case, back to England), we have updated our cottage to be more suited to full-time use and converted the old piggeries into a painting studio for Christopher and a storage space for belongings that don't fit into our cottage (which is smaller in square footage than our New York apartment!).

We have also joined two sheds together to make a small guesthouse (which we often rent out for additional income) and are just now beginning to think about converting the big old grain barn into a kind of gathering space for larger family meals. I'm campaigning to stretch out and live in the barn ourselves, eventually turning the cottage over to our rapidly growing teenagers, but Christopher can't quite get his head around that idea yet. We'll see. For now it's just going to be a place to expand into a bit—a Ping-Pong room for the kids; a larger boot room containing Christopher's outerwear for every possible sport, occasion, chore, and weather (yes, my coat and boot racks are both a quarter the size of his!); and a larger kitchen and dining space for entertaining.

Our living room, photographed on a particularly tidy day for Architectural Digest. *The red chairs are pretty ancient George Smith ones, and the antique chesterfield sofa is covered in a Robert Kime stripe. I bought the herbarium specimens (surrounding the fireplace) at the Paris Flea Market.*

Opposite and this page: Two of my favorite paintings by Christopher both hang in our dining room.

And finally, in the house, we have Fay, who comes in a few days a week to help me keep the inside chores moving along. In New York, I used to spend the better part of my income on a small army of women to help keep the house immaculate, look after the kids, run errands, and make meals. I was very rarely home alone—in fact, it's hard to remember when I ever was. At the time it felt good to have company in keeping everything running, but now that we live a simpler life, and both of our children are at boarding school, the task of running a household is a fraction of what it used to be. Although I am so grateful to have the support of Fay, I am also happy to be busy enough with new projects and jobs that I don't worry so much about the house being perfectly tidy and on a schedule all the time. It feels good to fold the laundry, scrounge around in the pantry for a meal spur of the moment, listen to music while doing the washing-up, and have time alone with Christopher or even on my own to enjoy the coveted silence.

The dining area and front entrance of our guesthouse. In contrast to our cottage, which is filled mostly with English antiques, the look of this house is more focused on Danish midcentury modern architecture and furniture mixed with the rustic nature of English farm buildings.

Our cottage kitchen, the place where I happily spend the most time. I am completely in love with my Lacanche cooker. It cost us a fortune but has proven its worth.

CHAPTER I—JUNE

Abundance of daylight – Dinner in the garden – Herb beds – Elderflower –
Christopher's passion for the farm – Strawberries – Radishes – Arugula –
The treehouse – Coco's riding – First hay harvest – Summer solstice

THE abundance of daylight is the defining characteristic of June. The early-morning sun, when not obscured by clouds, comes pouring in through our bedroom curtains just after four-thirty a.m. and shines through until nearly ten o'clock at night. It is pure joy! When we first moved here, I had to have the children's curtains relined with blackout fabric so that they could fall asleep on school nights when the sun was still high enough in the sky to brighten their rooms.

THE BEES OF JUNE FIND ALL HER ROSES SWEET,
AND SHE HAS NEW-MOWN HAY BENEATH HER FEET.

"Calendar," Teresa Hooley, 1949

Dizzy (aka Fatboy) being a total poser in front of the allium and centaurea montana (aka knapweed).

A much-coveted summer family meal alfresco. From left to right: Zach, Caroline, Coco, and Christopher.

On weekends, and even more so once the school year is finished, our whole schedule shifts to later in the day. We often get so caught up in what we're doing in the garden or the stableyard that we don't get around to cooking dinner till nine p.m. When we're lucky, on a clear night we can eat outside under the twinkling lights hung along the outside of the cottage. The kids hit a cricket ball around the yard with Christopher, and I have another glass of rosé while chatting with my mother-in-law, Caroline, the matriarch of the Brooks family. She often has supper with us, having lived on her own for more than forty years since her husband died, and she is excellent company—charming, witty, extremely knowledgeable on countless subjects, and the least judgmental person I think I've ever met.

Those warm evenings are some of the best moments of the year on our farm, and I have come to value them, as they aren't exactly typical of an English summer. Equally likely is that it's too chilly or wet to eat outside even once in the whole month of June.

With the extra sunlight in the day, we get a lot more done in the garden in June. I fill in the herb beds with annuals like flat-leaf parsley and cilantro, and there are plenty of flowers to cut—allium, sage blossoms, and honeysuckle are my favorites—to brighten up the house on the inside. I'm also consumed by elderflower in June. We have a huge tree in our garden and many more around the farm, especially down the hill near the field where the pigs live. Once they put out their lacy white blossoms, they are ready to be picked, soaked, and mixed with sugar and lemon juice to make Elderflower Cordial, a typical English syrup you can add to anything from sparkling water to a gin fizz. I make as many bottles as I can and give them out as gifts when we go to someone's house for a meal. I guess it's kind of odd that as the American girl from the big city I'm giving out a very amateur version of a typically English recipe to typically English people, but so be it. I enjoy it.

Our outdoor dining area, tucked up cozily against the cottage. We try to make it comfortable and welcoming without getting too precious. We live on a farm, after all.

Picking elderflower blossoms at the edge of middle Fairgreen field.

Elderflower Cordial

Adapted from Elisabeth Luard's
A Cook's Year in a Welsh Farmhouse

Fills two 1-liter bottles

18–20 elderflower heads, picked on a dry day before the heads droop

2 unwaxed lemons, juiced and thinly pared
4 cups water, brought to a boil
5 cups granulated sugar

As you are picking the elderflower heads, shake them vigorously to remove any debris or insects. Put the flowers and lemon zest into a large bowl and add the boiling water. Cover with a dishcloth and leave to infuse for 24 hours, giving the bowl an occasional stir.

Strain through cheesecloth to remove any additional debris or insects. Discard the flowers. Transfer the infused water to a heavy pan with the sugar, and heat slowly over a low flame, stirring until all the sugar has dissolved. Add the lemon juice, bring back to a boil, then turn down the heat and simmer for 5 minutes.

Pour the cooled liquid into glass bottles (I like to use recycled ones from old condiments or cordials) that have been sterilized with boiling water. Seal firmly. The cordial is ready immediately. I most commonly mix a few tablespoons of cordial (depending on desired sweetness) in sparkling water and add a squeeze of fresh lemon juice for a refreshing summer drink. For a slightly more exciting option, add some gin, to your taste, for an Elderflower Gin Fizz.

The cordial will last a few weeks if kept refrigerated. To make one that lasts longer, substitute citric acid for the lemon juice, dissolving 1 teaspoon of citric acid in 2 teaspoons of water for 2 cups of cordial.

In the garden, Christopher and I have pretty gender-(stereo)typical roles—I'm much more involved with the flowers, herbs, and vegetables that grow in close proximity to the house, and he is much more involved with anything that requires a machine or a very large shovel. By the time the growth season reaches June, I am already tired of hearing the mower whizzing manically around the farmyard on a quiet Sunday morning. If we were paying a gardener to do the job, it would happen during the week when the racket wouldn't so obviously disrupt the peace. But mowing is arguably Christopher's greatest passion—he does it *all* himself, not just our own lawns around the house but also the orchard and the verges throughout the entire farmyard. Once the mowing is done, the strimmer comes out to tidy the edges along the garden beds and stone walls. I really am so grateful for all this free maintenance—anything involving order makes me very happy—but the strimmer is even louder than the actual mower, and sometimes I just get fed up and have to ask him to do it while we are out riding or doing errands. Anything involving a chain saw is also a favorite task of Christopher's, except that twice now he has accidentally exposed an active bird's nest while cutting back the hedges, and both times the mother bird was so freaked out by the exposure that she abandoned the nest, which is heartbreaking, especially for Christopher, as he *loves* birds. So we now do our best to check the hedges before Christopher gets in there to hack away. As you can probably tell, a good dose of drama precedes the bucolic country moments I first mentioned.

Christopher's composting outfit.

Christopher's cutting-back-and-spraying-stinging-nettles outfit.

Fresh-picked strawberries from the Fairgreen kitchen garden.

Throughout England, June is probably best known for being the month of strawberries. Boy, do the English love their strawberries. It feels like everywhere you go
in those early-summer weeks, you are served a bowl of fresh strawberries topped
with a generous scoop of double cream. Leading the enthusiasm for strawberries
in our house is the most English one of us, Christopher. But truth be told, we all
love them. We eat them much the same as the rest of the country—sliced fresh
and topped with a generous helping of cream. As with all the berries we grow, I
like to prioritize the nicest fruit for eating raw, then the second tier gets used in a
summery dessert like my American favorite, Strawberry Shortcake, and then any
leftover fruit gets used for preserving. Jam-making would be the obvious choice
for leftover strawberries, but I find it hard to get excited about making something
you can get an excellent version of pretty much anywhere. Instead, I like to make
shrub, a drinking vinegar used for mixing into sparkling water for a mocktail or
into champagne for a cocktail. (See my Raspberry Shrub recipe in the February
chapter, and please note that with strawberry shrub I use balsamic vinegar.)

Strawberry Shortcake
Adapted from Original Bisquick recipe

Serves 6

4 cups sliced fresh strawberries
¹/₂ cup sugar
2 ¹/₃ cups Original Bisquick mix
¹/₂ cup milk
3 tablespoons granulated sugar
3 tablespoons salted butter, melted

whipped cream:

1 cup heavy cream
1 teaspoon vanilla extract
1 tablespoon confectioners' sugar

Mix strawberries and ¹/₂ cup sugar; set aside. Heat oven to 425°F.

Stir Bisquick mix, milk, sugar, and butter until a soft dough forms.

Drop 6 spoonfuls onto an ungreased cookie sheet.

Bake 10–12 minutes or until golden brown.

While biscuits are in the oven: In a large bowl, whip heavy cream until stiff peaks are just about to form. Beat in vanilla and 3 tablespoons sugar until peaks form. Make sure not to overbeat because the cream will become lumpy and butterlike.

Split shortcakes with a knife; fill with strawberries and top with whipped cream.

A more recent garden discovery has been radishes. They are easy to plant and easy to grow. When they first poked up through the dirt, however, I had no idea what to do with them. I didn't think I liked radishes, only planting them for Coco, who is a fan. But she was away at boarding school when they emerged, and I didn't want to see them go to waste. So I mentioned my lack of enthusiasm and direction on Instagram, and in the way that only Instagram is so miraculous, my followers wrote back with endless suggestions. I tried the first one that sounded appealing: simply drag a raw radish through a cold pat of butter, dip it in a bit of Maldon sea salt, and pop it in your mouth. I know it's not the most original thing to do with a radish, but I *loved* it. I ate every single radish in the garden just like that, defiantly never trying any other preparation. What I always disliked about radishes was the very dry, lean spiciness of them, and butter supplied the perfect contrast—a hunk of fat to balance the sharp flavor. I've also discovered how delicious their leaves are, just easily sautéed with oil and garlic. I plant radishes every spring now so I can harvest them in June and eat them all exactly the same way.

Radishes right out of the raised beds in our cottage orchard.

Arugula Salad

This is my own very simple recipe and one that can be served next to almost any meal or with the addition of avocado to eat as a meal in itself. Of course, it tastes best when the salad leaves are fresh from my garden, picked and washed just minutes before serving, and June is the height of that moment.

arugula
extra-virgin olive oil
balsamic glaze (I prefer its sweeter flavor
*   and sticky texture to normal balsamic*
*   vinegar)*

Ottolenghi Seeds for Salad (or make your
*   own using flaked almonds, pumpkin*
*   seeds, black sesame seeds, white sesame*
*   seeds, nigella seeds, chili flakes, Maldon*
*   sea salt, and extra-virgin olive oil)*
avocado (optional, for a heartier salad)
sea salt and black pepper

I use a large handful of leaves per person and then add avocado, dressing, and seeds according to taste. I start with slicing the avocado, usually about ¹/₂ per person, and then just before serving I drizzle a little oil and balsamic glaze and then sprinkle the seeds and salt and pepper over it at the very end.

The view of my office, converted from an old woodshed. Believe it or not, we don't have a gardener. Christopher does all the planting, weeding, maintenance, pruning, and mowing himself, with an occasional helping hand from me.

One of the highlights of our arrival here in June of 2012 was the addition of my office and the kids' treehouse. We had been at the farm in March of that year for spring break, and knowing that we'd soon be making the big transatlantic move, Christopher set those two building projects into motion. My office was a coming-to-England present of sorts from my very sweet husband, who knew I would need a place to work and also a place of my own where husbands and children weren't allowed in to mess up the tidiness and appreciation of order that is singular to me in our family. He gutted an old woodshed just three steps across a small gravel courtyard from the house and put in reclaimed oak floors, a charming old Jøtul wood-burning stove, and then whitewashed the existing rustic stone walls. He even furnished it for me, buying a beautiful Danish rosewood desk, a black-leather-and-walnut desk chair, and a teak credenza, all midcentury modern in style. I have since added an antique Moroccan rug, some vintage lamps, and a whole bunch of art that feels personal to me. I use it year-round, and it is heaven.

My office assistant, Eartha Kitten, asleep on the job.

Gingy the intern, far more eager.

The cottage garden treehouse in all its glory.

Zach, taking a shortcut down from the treehouse on the fireman's pole.

Probably the tidiest the treehouse interior ever was, when I tried to convert it to an art studio. Didn't last long.

The treehouse is also a showstopper. It's suitably rustic, sturdily built, and charming as can be. June is the best month for it too—the ash tree on which it is built is in full fresh-green splendor, the red poppies are usually blooming below, as is a bright pink dog-rose bush nearby. The whole scene is lush, idyllic, and endearing. These days the kids have nearly outgrown it—they go up there every once in a while, mostly when they have a friend over who's curious about it, the highlight being when Coco and her friend Edie actually slept the night in there once. But beyond that, it just kind of sits there begging to be admired from afar. Occasionally Christopher and/or I will climb up to the "crow's nest," a lookout point from the very top that gives a view of the entire farmyard. It's a unique view, and with lovely light at sunset, and I often scramble up there to snap a photo. One summer we gave the interior of the treehouse a bit of a refurb—putting a fresh coat of paint on the window frames and filling the "desk" area with art supplies. I thought it would make a nice little creative art studio—but again, the novelty wore off quickly, and it soon returned to just being a cool thing that people stop to stare at from the nearby bridle path. Still, I'm so glad it's there.

*The sweetest room in our home. It was first decorated by Christopher's sister
when she lived in the cottage for a brief stint. It was then inhabited and updated
(by way of rosettes) by Coco, but she outgrew it, and it is now a guest room.*

Coco galloping to the finish line of the Heythrop Team Chase. This is by far the scariest day of my year, watching her fly over big hedges at top speed (it's a race).

At the start of the summer, around when Coco arrives home from boarding school, her riding habits move away from hunting training (more on that in the November chapter) and become focused on riding at home and going to local competitions. Coco is by far the most active and passionate rider in our family. She has been on a horse consistently since age two, and she never doesn't want to ride. She keeps her mare Tottie at school with her and usually rides five or six days a week. I would say that so far riding is the greatest passion of her life, and I am grateful that she has such a focused interest. There is a way that Coco carries herself when riding—self-possessed, confident, and quietly in charge—that is unique to her being mounted on a horse. Of course there is frustration too, but when she and the horse are working together, I feel a surge of emotion and pride from watching them. I am also keenly aware of the dangers of Coco riding at the level she does, and I tell myself that, through the thousands of hours spent learning how to ride correctly and safely, she has earned the right to take the risks that she takes. Not that it's any less scary to watch.

On the farm, the harvest gets under way in June, starting with the first round of hay making, which we use for winter fodder (eating) for our horses. By the end of November, grass stops growing because of the shorter daylight hours and the colder temperatures, making it necessary for the horses to eat hay, whereas the sheep get by just fine on winter grass in their paddock. A horse's digestive system is tricky: they need to eat all day long, so you have to produce food they can eat all day long. We do give the horses some hard feed in the winter to boost their nourishment if they are working hard, such as while hunting or eventing. We also buy sacks of carrots and put molasses in their feed for additional vitamins and/or calories.

If the summer weather is fair, it's possible to get two crops of hay in the harvest season. You'd hope to get the first cut in late May or early June, and another in July or August. The critical part when the hay is cut is that it is able to dry flat on the ground, and in order to dry completely it needs to be turned over at least once. With the unpredictability of the British climate, this is always a stressful time, as the process of cutting it, drying it, baling it, and stacking it takes at least five days. There are very few periods in the English

Christopher checking up on the hay harvest in middle Fairgreen field.

summer when you get five straight days of dry weather. A heavy rain during this process has the potential to ruin the whole crop. If the spring and early summer has been typically wet and cold, there may be time to harvest only one crop.

The end of June, after the summer solstice, always feels sad to me, knowing that the days are already getting shorter. Sometimes the dark, gloomy winter months feel interminable, and during that time we console ourselves by imagining the long days ahead. But by the end of June, when summer is just getting going, the days are already getting shorter and it's a sober reminder of how short-lived that wonderful time is. I try to acknowledge the feeling once or twice, I might mention it to Christopher, and together we appreciate how good it feels to have such expansive hours of sunlight. Then we move on, with lots of time left to enjoy the rest of the summer, the still-long days, and hopefully (hopefully!) some sunshine and warm weather as well.

A young racehorse foal eating grass in front of the circle of trees that Christopher's father, Robert, planted in 1976, the year he died.

CHAPTER II—JULY

*Hound exercising – Pony Club – Thunderstorms – Winter-planted harvest – Picnics –
Flower arranging – In the orchard – Garden peas – Coco's birthday –
Escape to New York*

M Y favorite thing about July is when Christopher and I wake at dawn, load our road bikes into the back of the old Land Rover, and meet our local hunt to go out hound exercising. It's a great workout, much less scary than hunting, and a healthy and exhilarating way to start the day. The huntsman leads the pack of hounds at the front, and we all follow behind, typically around forty of us. The hunt staff wear tweed caps and simple khaki overcoats—kind of like a pared-down mac with a split in the back to make sure it falls neatly over the seat. It's a great look. I always think how my fellow fashion friends would freak out to see men dressed in such an authentic way, and so beautifully at that!

JULY WEARS SWEET PEAS TWINED AMID HER HAIR,
AND IN HER HARVEST ROBE RED POPPIES FLARE.

When it's a nice day, that warm, early sun hitting my face feels so good, and my heart gets pounding from working hard to pedal up the Cotswold Hills. The group of us is usually invited to the house where the meet was hosted for a bacon sandwich and a strong cup of coffee afterward. We have a great time chatting and watching the adorable and exhausted hounds cool themselves off in the nearest water trough.

Some hounds like to be noticed more than others.

Foxhunting in England

Originating as a sport in England in the early sixteenth century and continuing in much the same fashion until traditional hunting was deemed illegal in 2004, a pack of foxhounds would chase a fox's scent across the countryside with the purposing of catching and killing the fox. This activity would be followed by a field of men on horses following and watching the chase. Farmers and landowners pursued and supported this activity primarily as a means to reduce the number of young lambs killed by hungry foxes on land where sheep farming was the primary source of income and secondarily as a means of exercise and outdoor activity in the dreary winter months. Now that the killing of foxes has been banned, the hunt is much the same except that the hounds follow a trail of animal scent laid down in advance instead of chasing an actual fox. Regardless, the hunt is still called "the hunt" even though they are no longer hunting an actual animal. For more on hunting, go to page 171.

Our huntsman leading the way with the hounds as we exercise them on bikes in the early morning.

Christopher's sister Annabel at Heythrop Pony Club in the early 1970s.

Jumping was and is the main activity at Pony Club camp. They focus on it at all ages and at all levels. I suppose it's to prepare the kids to eventually start hunting. It's fun to see what they do but also scary to watch.

July is also the month of Pony Club, the highlight of Coco's summer since she was six years old. For one week, Coco spends nine a.m. to four p.m. each day doing everything you can possibly imagine on a horse.

The kids at Pony Club practice the typical things, like dressage, show jumping, and cross-country, but they also ride their horses through lakes, learn to jump with no stirrups, have grooming competitions, and listen to local professionals advise them on their future riding careers and hobbies, whether that be hunting or eventing. Both my least *and* most favorite part of the week is when the kids play "Chase Me Charlie," a game where everyone begins jumping a modest-height fence, which is then raised higher and higher each subsequent round. If your horse refuses, or you fall off, or you knock

Little Coco (with Sailor) at Heythrop Pony Club in 2009.

the fence down, that's it, you're out. As a parent watching, I am at once terrified and *excited*! I'm always left slightly in awe, as no one would ever allow children to do something so dangerous in America. But here we are in England, where the riding culture is so much more pervasive, and the kids just love it.

One year, when Coco was twelve, they did the whole game bareback, and she won it, jumping 4-feet-3 with no saddle or stirrups. She's got nerves of steel, my daughter, which makes me both proud and daunted. On the final day of camp, the parents come for the afternoon and the kids show off everything they have learned that week. There are lots of rosettes to go around, and over the years, Coco has won prizes ranging from "Most-Willing Pony" and "Best Turned-Out Horse" to "Most Improved." It is the sweetest week—all these rosy-cheeked young kids (mostly girls) in their tweed jackets, dedicating themselves to something about which most of them are entirely passionate, some less so. It's wholesome, challenging, and fun. And *so* English.

I dreaded the day when she would tell me she had grown out of it, and that day finally arrived at age fifteen when she chose to go to Greece for a week with a friend instead of going to Pony Camp. Boo-hoo.

*Megan getting some love and reassurance
from Po after her big accident.*

July brings thunderstorms here on the farm, which, since one particularly scary incident, makes me more concerned than I used to be. A couple of years back, there was a lightning storm *all freaking night long.* It was Coco's first night back from boarding school, so we decided I would have a sleepover with her in her room. We hardly slept—it was as if someone kept flashing the lights on and off, over and over again—it was endless. Ginger, who never jumps up on a bed when people are in it (must be one of her rescue dog neuroses), was right there in the bed with us, her body pressed hard against mine and shaking manically—think Scooby-Doo. I wasn't really worried about anything apart from whether we'd have any electricity in the morning. As the sun rose, I went down to make the coffee (we had power!) and saw a text from our groom, Sinead, saying that Megan, my brother-in-law's hunter, was hurt and I needed to call the horse hospital immediately. As I picked up the phone, I sent Christopher outside to investigate, and I soon followed behind. Megan was outside of the fenced-in field where she lives, and she was lying down in the grass. I looked up to check on the others (she's usually in a field with at least four other horses), and I noticed that a section of the metal fence surrounding the field was *entirely* flattened. It appeared that the lightning had spooked Megan and she'd run literally right *through* the iron fence. It wasn't clear whether she hadn't seen it in the dark or she was just so scared that she charged on through it. As I looked back toward Megan, she was now standing up but not putting much weight on one of her back legs—not a good sign. While Sinead was trying to get her to walk around a bit, I went over to check on the other horses. Coco's horse, Jake, was also cut up pretty badly on his legs. We don't know if he tried to follow Megan over the fence or he had his own incident. I led him into the stables to get him bandaged up and, on the way, saw that Megan was—thankfully—now walking, albeit slowly, but using both back legs. I got a call back from the horse hospital saying that a vet was on the way, and I told dispatcher that I thought Megan's big cut could likely be stitched up on-site. I had to run off then for an event at Zach's school, and when I returned a few hours later, both horses had had their injuries treated and were declared to be heading toward recovery.

The metal fence that Megan flattened. Still can't believe it.

We were so lucky to have averted any real disaster. This wasn't the first time a horse was injured on our farm, but it was a particularly scary one. Mostly I was amazed at the sheer strength of Megan to run straight through a metal fence. Sometimes I have taken riding horses for granted, but every now and then something like this comes along and simply humbles me.

Elsewhere on the farm, the harvest gets into full swing. Oilseed rape, one of the main crops on our farm, tends to come first in July. The seeds (they look like extremely fine green beans) that it produces are crushed and then used to produce vegetable oil (we Americans call this *canola oil*). Again, timing is key here to get a good weather window for the harvest before the seed becomes too ripe and falls out of the pod.

Next come the cereals: winter-planted wheat, followed by oats, barley, and then the spring-planted wheat. *Winter wheat* means it has been seeded after the harvest in September or October and starts its growth pattern before the frost of winter, so it subsequently grows faster than the spring sowing. This means that at harvest time there is a staggered cycle of crops coming ripe. It helps not having to harvest everything at the same time. We sell these crops, and their use generally depends on their quality, varying from animal feed to flour for bread.

A field of our wheat in its midsummer growth cycle.

Straw is the by-product of wheat, barley, or oats, and it is used for bedding for our horses, with the excess sold to other farms for their livestock bedding. When the crop is ripe, the combine harvester separates the ears of the cereals from the stem and throws the discarded stems back out onto the stubble to dry in the sun and eventually be baled and stored. In years gone by, we would burn the excess because the ash is fertile, but there was a general consensus that insect life was adversely affected, so this is no longer the practice.

We burn much of our paper and cardboard refuse, and Zach loves to build a bonfire with Christopher in the orchard.

A picnic with family friends at a nearby farm.

Not that there is any reliably good month in which to picnic in England, but if I had to make the safest bet, I would shoot for July. It's funny: the English seem to be very enthusiastic picnickers despite the mercurial weather. They even picnic at the opera while wearing black tie! (Which sounds totally unappealing to me. Who wants to schlep—and then handle!—all that food in a gown?) Nonetheless, picnicking is a thing here, and I try to join in when a suitable occasion presents itself. Sometimes we put a packed lunch—Scotch Eggs being imperative (see page 88 for recipe)—in a backpack and set off on the horses to find a nice place with a view or by the nearby lake to sit and eat. Typically, I'm either walking or running or riding around the farm, so I don't take the time to really *look* all around me. A picnic is a very welcome change of pace in that regard. Other times, we'll go sit by a pond with family friends where we can swim if we feel like it. (Though come on now, warm enough to swim? That's just being greedy.) I do love an afternoon spent in the woods just near our cottage—especially when the bluebells are out, but that happens earlier in the summer in May, when the weather is even less reliable.

Having supper alfresco is only slightly less rare in July than it is in June, but we grab every chance that we can to enjoy a meal in the garden even if the weather is only borderline acceptable. When we used to spend our summer weekends on Long Island, I got into the habit of cooking certain favorites and I have re-created them at the farm to give myself and the kids a nostalgic sense of continuity even though our lives are now vastly different.

Scotch Eggs
Adapted from Felicity Cloake for *The Guardian*

Makes 4

6 eggs total, 4 in shell for boiling
¹/₂ pound plain sausage meat
¹/₂ pound ground pork
3 tablespoons chopped mixed herbs
 (I like chives, sage, parsley, and thyme)

pinch of ground nutmeg
1 tablespoon English mustard
splash of milk
¹/₃ cup flour
2 cups panko bread crumbs
vegetable oil, for cooking

Put four of the eggs into a pan, cover with cold water, and bring to a boil.

Turn down the heat and simmer for 5 minutes, then put straight into a large bowl of iced water for at least 10 minutes.

Put the meat, herbs, nutmeg, and mustard into a bowl, season to taste with sea salt and black pepper, and mix well with your hands. Divide into 4 portions.

Carefully peel the eggs. Beat the 2 remaining raw eggs together in a bowl with a splash of milk. Put the flour in a second bowl and season to taste with salt and pepper, then tip the bread crumbs into a third bowl. Arrange in an assembly line.

Put a square of plastic wrap on your work surface and flour lightly. Put one of the

meatballs in the center, and flour lightly, then cover with another square of plastic wrap. Roll out the meat until it's large enough to encase an egg, and remove the top sheet of plastic wrap.

Roll one peeled egg in flour, then place in the center of the meat. Bring up the sides of the film to encase it, and smooth it into an egg shape with your hands, covering the egg entirely with the sausage mixture. Dip each egg in flour, then egg, then bread crumbs, then egg, then bread crumbs.

Fill a large pan a third full of vegetable oil and heat to 350°F (or when a crumb of bread sizzles and turns golden, but does not burn, when dropped in).

Cook the eggs, a couple at a time, for seven minutes, turning to cook evenly until crisp and golden, and drain on paper towels before serving.

DAD'S HALF-SCRAMBLED EGGS
WITH CREAM CHEESE AND CHIVES

My dad hated to cook. Ever since I was around ten years old, when my older sister and I went to stay with him, he made us a deal. He would buy the groceries and do the dishes, but we would be expected to do the bulk of the cooking. He had a few exceptions, things he not only enjoyed preparing but prided himself on doing well. Perhaps the most memorable of those recipes was his scrambled eggs. These days, when I miss him (he died in 2016), I make his eggs in my own farm kitchen and feel his presence so strongly.

SERVES 1

salted butter, for the pan
3 eggs
1 1/2 teaspoons cream cheese

chives, chopped
sea salt and black pepper

Crack three eggs (per serving) into a buttered frying pan over medium-low heat. While the eggs are slowly cooking, dab a little cream cheese (about 1/2 teaspoon per egg) evenly over them. When the egg whites look about half-cooked, use a fork to scramble the eggs while in the pan. Finish cooking so that both whites and yolks are slightly firm. Sprinkle with chopped chives and salt and pepper to taste. Serve with buttered fresh white toast.

VIVEKA'S SWEDISH PANCAKES

Growing up in Bronxville, my best friend Alexandra's Swedish mother, Viveka, used to make us pancakes (which were actually more like crepes) as a treat on weekend mornings. The taste of them still takes me right back to childhood. Viveka used to serve hers with sour cream and apple sauce—delicious!—but over the years I have adapted it to a mixture of crème fraîche and raspberry jam, which is very popular in my family. This Sunday morning treat in our house has become as much of a tradition for my kids as it was for me as a child.

SERVES 4

3 eggs
2 ¹/₂ cups milk
1 ¹/₄ cups flour
salted butter, for the pan

1 cup crème fraîche
1 heaping tablespoon raspberry jam,
    or more to taste

Place a nonstick crepe pan over medium-high heat. While it's getting warm place the eggs, milk, and flour in the blender and blend until the lumps are smooth. Mix the crème fraîche and raspberry jam together in a bowl and set aside.

Melt the butter in the pan and then pour the batter in to make your first pancake. Getting the right amount takes some practice, as you want the pancakes to be thin like crepes. I pour straight from the blender and swirl the batter around in the pan until it looks about right. If this makes you nervous, start with a large ladle or cup measure and use about ¹/₃ to ¹/₂ cup of batter depending on the size of your pan. Don't worry, you'll get the hang of it. For some reason the first pancake is always a bit wonky, but they get much better as you go. Loosen the edges of the pancake with a plastic spatula and have a peek underneath once it starts cooking through. When the facedown side is nice and golden, flip the pancake.

When the pancake is golden on both sides, transfer it to a plate and serve with the raspberry crème fraîche. I let my kids pour their own amount of raspberry crème fraîche over the top, roll them up, and eat. Yum.

Nuno's Penne with Mozzarella, Tomato, Basil, and a Secret Ingredient (Anchovies)

Nuno and his wife, Muriel, are great friends of ours who live in New York. When we needed a break from the responsibilities of our own summer house, we would often go spend the weekend at theirs, and I was fascinated by watching Nuno, a passionate Italian, cook pasta. This is my favorite of the ones he taught me.

SERVES 4–6

1 pound penne pasta (I prefer De Cecco)
¹/₂ pound freshest cherry tomatoes, chopped in half
¹/₂ pound buffala mozzarella, cut into ¹/₂-inch cubes

handful fresh basil, hand shredded
olive oil
sea salt and black pepper
3 anchovy fillets in olive oil
Parmesan cheese

Bring a large pot filled with the pasta, water, and a big pinch of salt to a boil. Meanwhile, in a large bowl, combine the tomatoes, mozzarella, basil, a few glugs of olive oil, and salt and pepper. Let it sit.

In a large pan over medium heat, cook three anchovy fillets (or more if you like things salty) in a tablespoon of their own oil. Make sure to cover the pan with a lid or splatter guard, as the anchovies will spit! Remove from heat when it looks like the fillets have just disintegrated.

When the penne is al dente (usually 9–11 minutes, but follow the instructions on the package), strain the pasta and pour it into the frying pan with the anchovies. Stir well. Pour that mixture into the bowl of tomatoes and mozzarella, making sure to include all the anchovy bits. Stir well.

Add salt and pepper and freshly grated Parmesan to taste.

Note: This recipe can be served room temperature but not cold.

July is also the time of year when I get into a bit of manic flower arranging. There are so many pretty things popping up in the garden—roses, peonies, and philadelphus being among my favorites—and they are just too plentiful and pretty not to bring inside, especially when we have friends coming to stay. I have even been known to cram flower arranging into a busy schedule late at night, aided by a twinkling string of outside lights and—if I am lucky—a full moon. I set all the vases on the outdoor dining table close to the house, put on my headlamp, and get on with cutting, gathering, and placing the flowers where I want them to go. There's something magical about being in the garden late at night, by myself, with the stillness of the summer air and the light of the moon, creating something beautiful to share with friends.

Other times, I find myself arranging flowers for no particular reason at all other than to pleasurably distract myself from the stress of everyday life. Yes, even life on the farm can have its stressful moments. When I feel I've gotten too caught up in my e-mailing, or distracted by my kids, or overwhelmed by the prospect of starting from scratch on a new project, I often clear the decks and start again by cutting flowers in the garden. And like starting anything else new, I always get a twinge of anxiety because it's never obvious which flowers I am

Arranging flowers to welcome weekend guests.

going to pick or how I am going to put them together. Often one variety is in bloom, but there is not enough with which to make an entire bouquet. So I have to figure something else out that will look pretty to go along with them. This is actually more challenging for me than it sounds. For many years I have been a flower minimalist—I tend to like a handful of all the same variety of flower tightly and tidily arranged in a neat little uptight city-girl bouquet. But the country has made me relax. (A little.) My arrangements are looser, and I have learned to mix and match when necessary. I have also come to like the uneasiness I feel as I figure out what I am going to do. I realize that that subtle tension is a natural by-product of creativity, which makes the process more engaging and ultimately more satisfying.

Philadelphus.

One phenomenon that just appears in our garden entirely on its own every year is a spectacular explosion of red-orange poppies. They grow in a strange place, right in the middle of the lawn on the side of our house. It turns out there used to be a garden bed there, but when Christopher dug it out to enlarge the grass area, the poppies somehow remained and continued to flourish. So every late June or early July, they appear for no longer than a week or ten days. We wait and wait the whole year for them to bloom, and then they come and go in a flash. I take *lots* of photographs of them to help preserve the moment and remind myself how worthy the wait is.

In the orchard, where there are raised beds in between the fruit trees, our attention turns to gorging ourselves on peas. I'd ideally now share with you all the ways I have learned to

When I don't have time to make big arrangements, it's still worth the effort to put a single flower at my bedside.

I started collecting small jars (from vanilla extract, rose water, etc.) and one day had the idea to put one stem in each one down the table instead of making bigger singular arrangements. I'm into it.

Rosa "Blush Noisette."

Rosa "Constance Spry."

Rosa "Bleu Magenta."

Rosa "Maiden's Blush."

Rosa "Blush Noisette."

prepare them—soups, salads, risottos—except that in our family, those perfect little ripe green vegetables nestled so neatly into their pods never even make it into the kitchen. We eat them all raw, in the garden. Every single one of them. We just pick a big handful—Christopher most likely leading the way with multiple handfuls—plonk ourselves down in the grass, and eat until we can't eat anymore. None of us can imagine a better way to enjoy them.

July 6 is Coco's birthday, and it falls just around the time when school lets out for the summer. Ever since Coco was a tiny baby, we have had a little tea party in the garden to mark her big day. Until she was five, she had an ancient pony named Mr. Teddy, and the tradition was that she and Mr. Teddy would both dress up like fairies on her birthday. Good old Mr. Ted would be parked in the garden wearing a feathery tiara and sparkly wings, and Coco, similarly dressed, would sit on him for the duration of the afternoon. She would eat her cake and receive all her visitors and well-wishers from atop her beloved steed. Once, however, she made the mistake of tying a Mylar balloon to Mr. Teddy's head collar. Unfortunately, this was one step too far for the ever-patient Ted. Within a few minutes, he spooked terribly—rearing up, ripping the rope off the fence where he was tied, and then heading down the driveway in a full gallop. His field mate, Murphy, a loyal cob with feathery hooves, heard the commotion and caught up with Mr. Teddy on the other side of the hedge. They ran along together, headed straight downhill, until Murphy arrived at the cattle grid, which he then dangerously jumped in order to catch up with Ted in his state of distress. Both horses soon ran out of steam and were rounded up and put safely back in the field. Needless to say, Coco has never brought a balloon anywhere near a horse ever again.

In more recent years, as Coco has come into the possession of much less patient horses, they make fewer appearances at her birthday tea party (although old man Sailor did show up this past year), but we have a great time celebrating her in the cottage garden nonetheless. The biggest challenge is that Coco doesn't particularly like cake. She does, however, *love* almond croissants. So one year I ordered two dozen of them from a local French baker and piled them up to resemble the shape of a cake. I then decorated the whole thing with fresh raspberries, metallic stars, and sparkling candles. I think she was impressed. Another year I took a risk and made an actual cake—it was a Ferrero Rocher–flavored cake, and it had actual Ferrero Rocher chocolate on top. Coco is insane about Ferrero Rocher chocolates, so I thought making a cake from them was worth the risk. I still can't tell how much she actually liked it—she's too English (i.e., polite, reserved) to tell me if she didn't—but I could tell that, yet again, she was at least charmed by my effort.

The kids' playhouse all done up for Coco's big day. The shed has since been transformed into a chicken house and it's now a storage room for hot tub accessories.

Coco celebrating her fourth birthday in the cottage orchard with Mr. Teddy.

When we ride cross-country, we all wear serious crash helmets and chest protectors. Coco even wears an
airbag vest when she jumps big things. This is her hat, decorated with a jockey silk to make it look less technical.

In recent years Zach and I have left Coco and Christopher happily at home on the farm and escaped to New York City for the latter part of July. I always find I have some work to catch up on there, and I relish the chance to spend the days alone working in my home office in our apartment. For most of the year, our apartment is rented, as we rely on its income for living expenses, but I try to space out the tenants so we have those few weeks to stay there and do some upkeep at the same time. On the farm, despite being in this remote, private location, there is always someone around, whether in the house or just outside the farmyard, and there is a chore needing to be done—animals need to be fed, dinner needs to be made, the kids need help with homework. It's ironic to think I have to go all the way to New York City for uninterrupted privacy, at least during the day, but so be it. Zach enjoys city life and being at "home"—yes, it still feels like home to both of us—as much as I do. He is the member of our family who probably finds it hardest to live on the farm all the time. Even when we go to a big town like Oxford (I can't bring myself to call it an actual city), Zach leans his head back, exhales, and says, "I feel so much better being in civilization!" He loves the manic city energy, in contrast to the much slower pace of the farm, and he relishes the chance to catch up with his former nanny, who was with us for nine years, see his old friends, and also to make new friends at whichever day camp he chooses to go to that summer. So as my acknowledgment of our mutual love for our home city, and my gratitude for Zach's making the most of his life on the farm, we spend a dreamy two weeks in our own apartment, in our own beds, pretending that we are still New Yorkers. It makes us both so happy. And toward the end of the month, I am ready to get the hell outta there, feeling grateful that we have chosen to live more peaceful and civilized lives back in England.

CHAPTER III—AUGUST

Riding on stubble – Hot air balloons –
Harvesting through the night – End-of-summer stillness

TRUTH be told, I'm not here on the farm that much in August, except sometimes at the very beginning and usually at the very end of the month. It's a shame, really, as I would happily trade being here in August for being away in any month between January and April. But in my own family, two weeks of August are spent in the Adirondack Mountains of upstate New York, a tradition that goes back to when I was five years old.

I do, however, have memories of being here on the farm in early Augusts past, and Christopher and Coco always stay behind for the first week of the month before catching up with Zach and me in America. I love getting pictures from them of the full harvest moon and the bleached fields of wheat straw around the farm.

IN AUGUST FIELDS THE GOLDEN CORN SHEAVES RISE,
AND DAHLIAS ARE HERS, AND DRAGONFLIES.

For the past four years, I have found myself back on the farm for the last week of August, getting the kids settled in, recovered from jet lag, and ready to go back to school. The English August in my mind, and as it has been in reality for the past few years, is lovely and warm and *dry*. Having harvested the wheat and barley in the middle of August, the fields are filled with brittle blond stubble. It's the only time of the year when you can ride a horse straight over the fields without ruining a growing crop. During that last week, we often wake early to join the hunt in exercising the foxhounds—this time on horses. It's more of a fun ride than an organized hunting activity, and we all savor the freedom of cantering straight across miles of neat rows of stubble, with the hounds keeping up alongside us. It's a wonderfully free and romantic feeling, being unconcerned with sticking to a path.

If the month is indeed even a fraction as warm and sunny as one would hope, then the sky above the cottage is constantly filled with hot air balloons in the afternoons and evenings. Although I somehow managed to summon the nerve to take a ride in one in Colorado in my early teens, I have yet to find the courage to go up in one here, as amazing as it would be to float over the farm on a beautiful summer evening. So for now, I just enjoy the sight of those colorful balloons drifting peacefully in the breeze, up and over the fields and hills beyond.

I keep our meals in August pretty simple, bracing myself for the abundance of September in the orchard and all the cooking and preserving that requires. Before Coco heads back to boarding school, I make her favorite Salmon Stir-Fry dinner and Olive Oil Picnic Cake for tea. And the one thing I do on the preserving front is make syrup from the elderflower berries that have been harvested and frozen for me while I was away on my travels.

Our friend Miranda with her children, riding over the stubble. We always love the new perspectives and views that the brief window of being allowed to walk or ride over the fields allows us. The rest of the year it is forbidden to walk through them, as you would be potentially damaging a valuable crop.

SALMON STIR-FRY

SERVES 4

4 salmon fillets
sea salt and black pepper
2 tablespoons sesame oil
¹/₂ pound bok choy
¹/₂ pound shelled frozen edamame
¹/₂ pound broccolini

¹/₂ pound sugar snap peas
2 tablespoons mirin
1 ¹/₂ tablespoons oyster sauce
1 ¹/₂ tablespoons soy sauce,
*   plus more to taste*
12 ounces precooked egg noodles

Preheat the oven to 450°F. Season the salmon fillets with salt and pepper and place skin-side down on a nonstick baking sheet. Bake until the salmon is cooked through, 12–15 minutes.

    While the salmon is cooking, pour the sesame oil into a wok or large pan. When it is hot, add the green vegetables and stir constantly. Add the mirin, oyster sauce, and the 1¹/₂ tablespoons soy sauce. When the vegetables look nearly cooked, add the egg noodles and stir until heated through and they start to soften.

    Remove the salmon from the oven and place one fillet over each serving of stir-fry. Drizzle with soy sauce to taste.

OLIVE OIL PICNIC CAKE
Adapted from Elisabeth Luard's *A Cook's Year in a Welsh Farmhouse*

I'm not usually a big cake eater, apart from when I'm celebrating someone's birthday, but in the summer when we are doing chores or enjoying adventures outside, we all build up an appetite for teatime. Especially with dinner running so late during the longer days, it's lovely to sit in the garden (weather willing) with a slice of cake and a cup of our favorite Lapsang souchong tea in the late afternoon.

SERVES 6

1 1/4 cups all-purpose flour
2 teaspoons baking powder
7/8 cup granulated sugar
1/2 teaspoon sea salt

3 large eggs, beaten
6 ounces light olive oil
zest and juice of
* 1 unwaxed lemon*

Preheat the oven to 350°F. Line a loaf pan with waxed paper and brush with oil.

Sift the flour with the baking powder into a bowl and mix in the sugar and salt. Add the eggs, oil, lemon zest and juice and beat with a wooden spoon until the mixture is smooth and free of lumps. (This can be done in a food processor if you like.)

Tip the batter into the prepared pan, smoothing it into the corners. Bake for 45–50 minutes, until the cake is well risen, firm to the finger, and well shrunk from the sides. Run a knife around the sides and remove from the pan to cool on a wire rack.

Elderberry Syrup and "Fizz"
Adapted from Kevin West's *Saving the Seasons*

MAKES 4 CUPS

Syrup:

3 pounds elderberries
1 or 2 pods star anise

¹/₃ cup water
2 cups granulated sugar

Rinse the berry clusters and methodically strip them from their stems, which smell rank. Place the berries in a large pot with the star anise and crush with a potato masher. Add the water and bring to a boil. Lower the heat and simmer for 10 minutes, mashing the fruit several more times. Strain the juice through a damp jelly bag and let it hang until cool; then squeeze the bag to extract the remaining juice. You should have about 3 cups.

Bring the juice to a boil in a preserving pan and stir in the sugar. When the sugar has dissolved, ladle the syrup into sterilized bottles. Seal and store in the fridge for up to two months.

"Fizz":

Pour 2 tablespoons Elderberry Syrup into a glass over crushed ice. Add ¹/₄ teaspoon freshly squeezed lemon juice, and top up with ¹/₂ cup sparkling water. Rub the rim with a twist of lemon peel and then drop it in as a garnish. You can add some gin, too, if you feel like it!

*Zach, Poppy, Grey, and Coco taking in the new view from the top
of the straw bales. This year's was a particularly big harvest.*

Another hallmark of late summer, and typically the last week in August, is the sight and sound of tractors working through the night to finish harvesting the crops in the fields—usually wheat, barley, oats, oilseed rape, peas, and beans—while the weather is good. If they are working close to the house, I can see the headlights occasionally shine through my bedroom windows, and regardless of where the tractors are on the farm, I can almost always hear the engines running, sometimes until two or three in the morning. It's not an obtrusive sound, but there is a rightness to its purpose that would make me tolerant even if it were.

I find the whole notion of August—the stillness of time away from work, the winding down of an abundant season, the romance of the harvest, the last days of freedom—to be a dreamy time on the farm. This is especially so because in all the years of living in New York, the end of summer meant the end of country life, which always meant returning to rushed days, too many take-out meals, and constant exhaustion. After those summers, when I had spent time both in England and in the Adirondacks passing much of the day outside in nature, cooking meals for my family, and acclimating to a more manageably paced day, the reality of returning to the city was harsh. I would try to hold on to my country lifestyle for as long as possible—

waking earlier than normal to have a bike ride along the river before work, ordering groceries on a Sunday so that I could more easily cook meals during the week, and trying to schedule fewer social nights out—but I would sooner or later inevitably return to the constant buzz and movement of the city and long for summers in the country once again. It is the memory of that feeling that inspires gratitude at the end of the summer, that this country life we have built is now our focus. While I do occasionally long for that New York fix—and I do give myself permission to have it—the balance of city versus country has been reversed in a way that has brought more meaning and fulfillment to my life and that of my family.

Malva moschata, *more commonly known as musk mallow, in the front bed of the cottage garden.*

January

February

March

July

August

September

Sometimes Coco tells me that I Instagram pictures of the garden shed too much, but I don't think that I do. To me, it looks different every single day of the year, and I enjoy documenting that. It is the most romantic building, especially because it really is a garden shed—filled with pots, gardening tools, weed killer, lanterns, soil bags, the lawn mower, etc. Despite pleas from many friends, we haven't converted it into

April

May

June

October

November

December

a small guesthouse or some other renovated structure. There is a fireplace inside (as evidenced by the chimney) that is no longer used, which does make it tempting to transform the shed into some kind of cozy, inhabited room, but Christopher is adamant that sometimes a shed should just remain a shed. He resists the idea of living in a farmyard where everything is pristine and quaint. I can't say that I disagree, tempting as it is sometimes.

CHAPTER IV—SEPTEMBER

*Back to work – Jam making – Fruit harvest (pears, figs, blackberries) – Easy meals –
Fresh eggs – Hedge trimming – Hay bales – Back to school – Living in close quarters –
Writing habits – Riding in the fog – Zach's birthday*

I find that when I return to the farm after a day or two away, it always feels welcoming and idyllic, and I am so grateful to be here. If I have been away for a longer period, however, especially in the summer when I am often away for five or six weeks at a time, I almost inevitably arrive back to the farm with a distinct "What the hell am I doing here?" feeling. Those first few days are kind of like the first few days of a holiday: it takes a while to slow down and settle in. Whatever energy I have acquired from my travels needs to dissipate and get teased out of my nervous system. Good weather is miraculous in speeding up this tedious process, but even in the cold, cloudy drizzle, I eventually reenter the country vibe and once again feel certain this is where I am meant to be.

September is a *huge* month on the farm. Even though the summer is officially over, the abundance of fruit and subsequent cooking, preserving, and baking I do moves into full swing. For me, it's not an easy month to be so domestic because, after the long summer holidays have ended and the kids have gone back to school, my own driven, overly motivated New York City brain, even after all this time, tells me it's time to get back to work. And no matter how I justify it, making Pear Compote and Fig Jam will never, ever feel like work to me. So instead I toil away in my office during the week, feeling like I'm doing whatever more serious stuff I am meant to be doing—writing, blogging, consulting, or paying bills—and then on the weekend I get into serious "farmer's wife" mode in the kitchen.

SEPTEMBER NUTS AND BLACKBERRIES ARE GOOD,
WHILE ROBIN SINGS FROM OUT THE YELLOWING WOOD.

The typical result of a September fruit-preserving-frenzy weekend.

Jam/jelly/compote making is an art, not a science. The first time I attempted to make jam—from the coveted last few homegrown blackberries of the season—I followed the recipe to the letter but ended up with something that more accurately resembled hard candy than jam. I underestimated how long it takes to reach the near setting point only to get distracted at the crucial moment and ended up past the setting point. I have since read many jam-making books and recipes and only now feel I am starting to truly understand the process and recognize the crucial moments. The best 101 guide I've discovered is Kevin West's *Saving the Season*. In it you will find a recipe for preserving nearly any fruit you can imagine, and the eight-page intro at the beginning is the best tutorial on the subject that I have found.

Laura Bailey's Pear Compote

Laura is a wonderful friend from my early New York days when we were both in our twenties. We shared so many formative experiences together—Sunday morning trips to the flea market, fretting over boyfriend issues, and going to our first fashion shows, both of us thrilled and intimidated. She was even a bridesmaid in my wedding to Christopher. Laura now lives in England, too, which has brought us to a whole new and more grown-up chapter in our friendship. Nothing confirmed this more than when I went to visit her country house one weekend and she gave me homemade Pear Compote from fruit grown in her orchard. I'd never had Pear Compote before and it sat in my pantry for a few months before I felt inspired to open it. When I finally did, I poured a few spoonfuls of it over sheep's milk yogurt and Ottolenghi granola and was instantly hooked—and inspired! I had at last found something desirable to do with the abundance of pears that ripen in our farmyard each early summer. I now consider Pear Compote a Fairgreen Farm perennial.

Makes six 8-ounce jars

2 pounds pears, peeled, cored, and diced
   (weight measured after chopping)
1 1/2 cups granulated sugar

juice of 1/2 lemon
1/2 cup water
1/2 teaspoon ground cinnamon

Bring everything to a boil for 10 minutes and then simmer slowly for 60–90 minutes, until the pears are soft. Blast them with a hand blender until the texture is smooth. Pour the mixture into sterilized jars and seal. Simmer in a pan of water for 30 minutes.

Of course there are the less committed weekday pleasures as well: I eat figs and/ or autumn raspberries for breakfast nearly every morning for six weeks from early September to mid-October—I just chop them up into whatever oatmeal, yogurt, or cereal I am having. The routine of walking outside in my pajamas to pick fruit straight from the tree for my breakfast—this is the fulfillment of the farm-life fantasy that motivated me to move here in the first place. From time to time, I'll also have an impromptu blackberry-picking session with Christopher— he *loves* blackberries and knowing how much he enjoys it, I make time to share this childhood pleasure with him. There is nothing he loves more than a fresh blackberry dessert.

The timing of picking figs for eating is crucial. If they're even a day past their prime I use them in jam or baking instead of eating them fresh.

FIG JAM
Adapted from Kevin West's *Saving the Season*

Fig Jam is the key ingredient that makes several of even my favorite things that much better. In the autumn, for an easy Saturday lunch, I make grilled cheese sandwiches with sourdough bread, Gruyère cheese, prosciutto, and Fig Jam. They are truly one of the finer pleasures. My other favorite is to stir a teaspoon or two into my pinhead oatmeal (made with whole milk) on a cold winter's morning. For me, Fig Jam is a cozy, wintry treat, and I make sure to preserve it well so it lasts me through the gloomiest months.

MAKES FIVE 10-OUNCE JARS

3 pounds ripe figs (mine are the Brown Turkey variety and I tend to use ones that are just past ideal ripeness for eating)

2 cups granulated sugar
3 tablespoons freshly squeezed lemon juice

Cut the stems off the figs and quarter them.

Combine the fruit, sugar, and lemon juice in a mixing bowl. Stir to combine, then cover with plastic wrap and place in the fridge for a few hours or overnight.

Pour the fruit-and-sugar mixture into a preserving pan and rapidly bring to a boil. Stirring constantly, reduce over high heat until the hot jam has thickened, 6–8 minutes, then lower the heat to medium, and reduce a few more minutes to gel point.

Ladle into 5 prepared 10-ounce jars, leaving ¼-inch headspace. Seal, and simmer in a boiling water bath for 10 minutes.

WILD BLACKBERRY CRUMBLE TART
Adapted from Claire Ptak's *The Violet Bakery Cookbook*

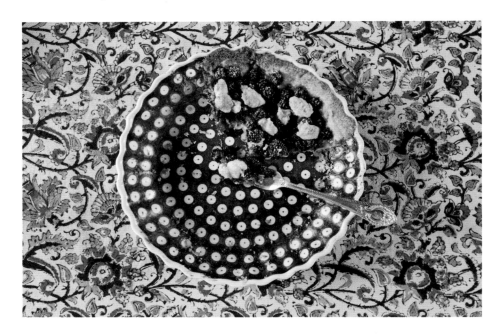

MAKES ONE 8-INCH TART,
WHICH CUTS INTO 6–8 SLICES

Pastry:

1 cup all-purpose flour
2 tablespoons granulated sugar
¹/₂ cup salted butter, softened
1 tablespoon white vinegar
butter, for greasing the pan

Filling:

¹/₂ cup granulated sugar
2 tablespoons all-purpose flour
1 teaspoon ground cinnamon
pinch of fine sea salt
1 pound fresh blackberries

Preheat the oven to 400°F. Butter an 8-inch tart pan.

Put all the pastry ingredients into a food processor and pulse briefly so that the mixture just comes together. Press all but 3 tablespoons evenly into the prepared pan (reserve the remainder to crumble on top) and set aside.

Mix together the filling ingredients, except the berries. Spread three-quarters of this mixture over the base of the tart. Toss the blackberries with the remaining dry mixture and tip onto the tart shell. Crumble the reserved pastry on top and bake for about 40 minutes until bubbly and golden. Serve immediately. Anything left over can be eaten the next day (even for breakfast). It's delicious cold.

Picking fruit is such a lovely activity to do together as a family. I find that fruit pickers fall into two camps: those whose picked fruit ends up in the bowl and those whose picked fruit ends up in their belly! Zach is definitely in the latter group.

My mother-in-law, Caroline, in the Fairgreen kitchen garden.

I also make a point of letting my mother-in-law know that I'll happily accept any kitchen garden leftovers from around the farm for making juices—she brings me mostly carrots and beets—and I mix them with apples or pears and ginger. Honestly, I am not a big juicing person—or a "raw" person—but making the occasional juice is an efficient way to make myself feel that I am being super healthy, even just for a second, and also not letting fresh, farm-grown produce go to waste.

One of the realities of living so rurally is that there is very little faking it when you don't feel like cooking. As city folks, Christopher and I were professional patrons of restaurants. All New Yorkers are, really, whether it be ordering in or going out to your favorite local Italian, Thai, or Japanese. Usually, the kids would already be fed by the time we got home from work, and we were both too exhausted by our long days in the city to feel like making dinner. It's not so much the cooking that was daunting but the planning of meals and buying groceries. Sometimes I'd be in the mood to cook, but the idea of thinking of what to make, the groceries it would require, and then standing on line to pay for it at a shop—or, even more daunting, planning ahead to order it online—just seemed like more effort than it was worth. This lazy attitude to eating at home really bothered me.

Now I'm faced with the opposite challenge: it took me a while to adjust to being responsible (my husband is *not* a cook) for every single meal not only for myself but for my family while on the farm. I especially notice it in September, when I am laying down so many hours in the kitchen preserving fruit that by the time it comes to meals, I am exhausted already.

Then again, there are two wonderfully positive benefits of not being able to fake it when you don't feel like cooking. First, with no choice but to make as many meals as I do, I have become a much better and more experienced cook. I still am not at the stage of regularly inventing new recipes off the top of my head, but I can make almost anything and often end up with my own version, making a confident tweak here or an addition there to whatever recipe I am following. Second, now that my kids are teenagers, they can pretty much fend for themselves when I occasionally—most often on a Sunday evening—announce that dinner is "every man for himself," meaning that I am excusing myself from the responsibility of cooking the family meal. The kids love the chance to make exactly what they feel like eating, typically relying on simple cheese quesadillas or pasta with tomato mascarpone sauce and grated Parmesan, usually eaten in front of the telly, and it forces them to learn a few cooking skills of their own.

When I do take on the family meals but don't have the time that day to make anything requiring a whole lot of forethought or planning, such as I would on the weekends, I turn to a few reliable favorites that can be easily cobbled together from what we have in the fridge and pantry, and they seem to please everyone.

We eat a lot of eggs on the farm, mostly because we have hens that lay them (one less thing to shop for!) but also because Coco is a vegetarian, and so it's one of the few protein sources we all like and can eat. I especially love omelettes because they work at every meal, and I can make them out of any leftovers/staples I have in the fridge and any herbs from the garden. The simple act of walking outside to pick herbs from my garden nearly makes leaving New York City behind worthwhile in and of itself. For me, it symbolizes one of the simplest and greatest pleasures of country living. Maybe if I'd had a few pots of fresh basil, parsley, and cilantro, I would have been able to tolerate city life for longer! But anyway, back to omelettes. As for the quantities, I always use three eggs per person, and the amount of additions are really just a matter of taste. In our family, Coco always likes extra cheese, and Zach prefers me to go light on the onions. So don't be too worried about quantities; just use your instincts.

JULIAN'S COMTÉ, RED ONION, AND CHIVES OMELETTE

Julian is Christopher's longtime friend and our most frequent houseguest. He's always welcomed by me because he's a great cook and he gives our kids lots of attention.

SERVES 1

3 eggs   *Comté cheese*
olive oil, for the pan   *chives, minced*
1 medium red onion, diced   *sea salt and black pepper*

In a small bowl beat the eggs with a fork.

Heat a medium pan until it is good and hot. (P.S. I don't use nonstick pans. In order to avoid sticking, just make sure your pan is heated through before even adding the oil to the pan.)

Add the olive oil to the pan, allow it to heat up, and then add the onion. With this recipe, Julian likes to simply sweat the onions as opposed to cooking them through. So just get them heated up a little bit before adding the egg to the pan. Grate the Comté over the omelette and then cover for a few minutes to cook through. When nearly done, sprinkle with plenty of chives and season with salt and pepper (as much as you like) to taste. Cook another minute or two and then remove from heat.

CHORIZO, POTATO, AND CHEDDAR OMELETTE

SERVES 1

3 eggs   *chorizo sausage, diced*
olive oil, for the pan   *Cheddar cheese, grated*
Vidalia onion (I use about one-third of a medium onion per person) *sea salt and black pepper*
any kind of leftover potatoes (or parboil and slice them if raw)   *fresh flat leaf parsley*

In a small bowl beat the eggs with a fork.

Heat a medium pan until it is good and hot.

Add the olive oil to the pan, allow it to heat up, and then sauté the onion for a few minutes until it's slightly brown and begins to soften. Add the potatoes and chorizo to heat through.

Add the egg to the pan. Just go ahead and dump it over what's already cooking. Sprinkle a small handful of cheese on top (this omelette is already quite rich, so not much cheese is necessary). Cover with a lid so the omelette cooks evenly. Just as it starts to look cooked through, use a spatula to fold the omelette in half. Season with salt and pepper and a sprinkle of fresh parsley to taste. Cook another minute or two and then remove from heat.

I never ate so many omelettes before I started making them with farm fresh eggs.
They taste so much better when they come straight from the hen.

CHICKEN TAGINE WITH BAKED CARDAMOM RICE
Adapted from Jane Coxwell's *Fresh Happy Tasty*

SERVES 3 (although I almost always double the recipe to make it for 6)

2 tablespoons olive oil
3 pounds boneless, skinless organic chicken
thighs, cut in half
1 teaspoon ground turmeric
1 medium red onion, cut into 8 wedges
2 garlic cloves, minced
¹/₂ thumb-size piece of ginger, minced

2 pinches saffron threads
sea salt
15-ounce can chickpeas
¹/₃ cup green olives, pitted and halved
juice from ¹/₂ lemon
agave nectar
¹/₂ cup roughly chopped cilantro
¹/₂ cup roughly chopped fresh flat-leaf parsley

Chicken Tagine:

Heat the olive oil in a large Dutch oven until smoking hot. Add the chicken pieces and give them time to get some good color on each side, about 2 minutes, untouched, per side. Lower the heat to very low and wait a minute for the pan to cool a bit, then add the turmeric. Cook for a minute to toast the spice—you'll know when it's done toasting because the smell intensifies.

Add the onion and stir for about a minute, then add the garlic, ginger, saffron, and a large pinch of salt. Add the chickpeas, including enough of their own liquid to cover all the contents plus about an inch. Bring to a boil, then lower the heat to simmer, cover partway with a lid, and cook for about 40 minutes, until you can see the chicken has started to become more tender and the whole mixture looks thicker and comes together.

Remove the lid and give the stew a good stir. Simmer for another 15 minutes, stirring occasionally. If it looks as though the pot is too dry, you can add a bit of water.

Add the olives and cook for 5 minutes. Turn off the heat and let it sit for a few minutes to rest. Add the lemon juice and season with salt and agave so that it's right for you. Finish with the cilantro and parsley.

Cardamom Rice:

SERVES 4

1 cup uncooked basmati rice
3 cardamom pods
2 tablespoons salted butter
1 bay leaf

sea salt
freshly ground black pepper
1/2 cup sliced almonds

Preheat oven to 350°F.

In an ovenproof dish, combine the rice, cardamom, butter, and bay leaf; season with salt and pepper and add 1 cup of water. Cover with foil and bake for about 40 minutes; check after 35 minutes, depending on your oven. You want the rice to soak up all the water but also to look dry.

In the meantime, toast the almonds in a small dry skillet over medium-low heat until golden brown, stirring often, 3 to 4 minutes. Set aside.

Remove the foil and gently fluff the rice with a fork. Check the seasoning, top with toasted almonds, and serve.

A late-summer view of Rickyard Cottage.

Christopher reliably gets back to his mowing in September, and the end of the summer season is marked by finally cutting the long grass that we let grow in the orchard during the warmer months. On a larger scale, the hedges all around the farm get cut back as well. There is a small window for this—after the harvest but before new planting so that the hedge-cutting machine can reach both the inside and outside of the hedge without damaging the crop. It's a bit sad to let go of the fullness of lush summer growth, but once the harvest is done, the grass is shorter, and the hedges are trimmed, the tidy new look on the farm overall provides its own satisfaction.

The kids also love the first month or two after the harvest, when hay bales are neatly piled high almost to the roof of the Dutch barn in our farmyard. They spend hours up there in their secret hideout atop the very tallest pile. God knows what they get up to, but their friends seem to like it as much as they do—they come over to hang out and all end up on top of the hay bales for hours and hours. They have even spent the night atop the hay bales once or twice! I try not to get too uptight about them coming back in the house trailing hay wherever they go, but inevitably I have lost my temper once or twice after they've ignored my pleas to strip down before coming back inside . . . it makes such a mess!

As the months progress and we've used the hay to feed the horses in the winter, the stack of bales gets smaller and more uneven. This is when the kids do less camping out up there and more jumping around from pile to pile, each now at a different height. It's not the safest thing to do—once Zach jumped from quite a high pile onto what he thought was a hay bale when it was really just a

*The aftermath of Christopher and Charlie's hay bale mishap. Richard Fudge came down
in another tractor to drag them out of the ditch, Charlie proudly posed in front of the disaster,
and Christopher took a moment to calm down with a cigarette!*

thick layer of hay covering the concrete floor. He bruised his heel and ended up
seriously limping for nearly a month afterward. We even took him to the local
medical clinic to get an X-ray—it was probably the one time that warranted his
going around on crutches for a while (isn't that every kid's dream?), but the clinic
had sadly run out of stock. Bad luck, Zach.

I figure there is worse trouble the kids could get into around the farm than playing
on hay bales, and there are plenty of stories to support that. The worst one happened when Christopher and his brother, Charlie, were Zach's and Coco's ages,
and they were already actively farming. Christopher was driving a tractor up the
driveway with his brother sitting dangerously on top of a *huge* pile of hay bales they
were hauling on a trailer at the back. Trouble was, the tractor had no brakes, so the
timing of Christopher's gear-shifting had to be perfect. Right when they were up
on the crest of the hill, Christopher had to downshift, and because the revs were
close to stalling, the lower gear wouldn't engage. The whole thing went careening
back down the hill and eventually jackknifed, throwing Charlie over the hedge and
into the field. It's a miracle they weren't seriously injured, let alone killed.

September is our time to get back into old routines or establish new ones. Christopher inevitably finds himself back in the painting studio after taking much of the summer off to focus his creative energy in the garden. He really loves the garden in a way that I can't imagine myself ever matching. Maybe I will when I am closer to his age! Zach and Coco are back to school, often at a new one, as we have found the case to be in England. The first two years we lived here, they both went to Kitebrook, the sweetest local school you can possibly imagine, set on a beautiful country estate in a grand old limestone house overlooking the best of the Cotswolds countryside. The students climbed trees and made forts in the woods during recess, cows watched from the sidelines as the kids competed on the sports fields, and everyone's parents and even grandparents were all lifetime friends. In fact, Coco's favorite teacher was her grandmother's goddaughter and Zach's was our next-door neighbor's sister! Christopher and his siblings went to Kitebrook, too, so Coco and Zach were embraced by the small, local community, had ample time to adjust to life in a new country and different style of teaching, and have made nearby friends for life. Then eventually Coco went off to boarding school and Zach started at a bigger day school. By the time this book makes its way to you, Zach will be joining Coco at her boarding school and who knows what I will do to fill the empty space and time at home. Just the thought of it fills me with panic.

There was a time when I wouldn't have thought it possible for Christopher and me to live happily together in England. Each summer when we paid our monthly visit to the farm, both before we had kids and after, I found Christopher to be more remote and distant than I was used to. After a week or ten days, I would often wonder to myself, "Where has my sweet and attentive husband gone?" and then we'd arrive back in New York at the end of our trip and within a week, he was completely back to normal again. Over the years, I mentioned it occasionally, and then one day he explained that there was emotional pain he associated with the farm—his father dying suddenly of cancer when he was a teenager, being sent off to boarding school at the tender age of eight, and the usual sibling and parental drama. He had moved to New York in his thirties to start fresh and evolved quite dramatically within his newfound freedom and separation from a painful past. Even though he longed to spend time on the farm for a good stint in the summer—often staying on longer after my job required me to head back to New York—he did feel that being there brought back a sense of melancholy that I was not used to being around. Over the years I reduced my time on the farm, from six weeks at the longest down to ten days when I was working at Barneys, partially to minimize the time I had to be around Christopher in his half-present state.

Coco leading in the hurdles at Kitebrook Sports Day.

Christopher and me, early morning, having our "Norman Rockwell" moment.

In considering our move to England, I brought up my reservations about his emotional well-being on the farm and suggested that he invest more time and energy into his life on the farm: perhaps he could make new routines, new memories, new friendships, and thereby create a new frame of mind. As we were planning on living on the farm for only a year when we first arrived, we felt that if things didn't improve, we could probably survive a year and then we'd go back to New York City, where we knew our relationship worked well.

As it turns out, with Christopher and me living on the farm together and being around each other all the time, as well as taking on more joint responsibilities, our marriage has evolved in both good and challenging ways. When we first moved to the farm, we were both so high, so bonded from the big, scary change we had taken on and agreed to together. Deciding to whittle a huge life with endless obligations and distractions down to a far simpler and more focused one felt incredibly intimate, committed, and romantic. Right from the start, when we arrived in England to begin a new life here, we were each on a path to define ourselves—Christopher in getting reconnected with farm life and me in creating it from scratch for myself. We were each on our own journey, albeit side by side, and we were at once supporting each other and getting to know each other all over again. It was wonderful. We each had our separate work spaces, mine in my office and his in his art studio, and then we would sit down to eat lunch together or take a break together in the afternoon to go pick blackberries for dessert that night. Sounds idyllic, right? Well, it was. Until it wasn't.

After a while, it was apparent that Christopher and I were spending perhaps too much time together. In order to maintain focus on our own agendas during the day, we learned to effectively ignore each other for much of the day, and that habit started to extend into the evenings, with my watching TV and reading in bed while Christopher spent late hours catching up on e-mails or trolling for things like reclaimed wood and Danish modern furniture on eBay. On the one hand, I am a strict morning person, often getting into the office by seven a.m., and have a disciplined habit of turning off my work around 6 p.m. Christopher, on the other hand, has a much slower start to his day and only gets going in his studio or with his work calls (especially the ones to America) in the evening. As you can see, this meant that one of us was always working and we didn't get to enjoy our downtime together. After such a blissful start, we soon found ourselves taking each other for granted and gasping for air in what had become a relationship that was at once claustrophobic and lonely: too much time together without enough fun.

It took us both a while to realize that changes needed to be made. For me, it was only after I had unintentionally found one solution that I realized more needed to be done to enjoy Christopher's company and feel grateful for his everyday presence in my life. In September 2014, Zach started at a new day school that was a forty-minute drive from our home. As I was driving so far, I was in search of a place nearby where I could write for the day so I wouldn't have to go back and forth twice. I figured out that it made sense to drive fifteen minutes away from the school into Oxford for the day. I got a reader's card at the Bodleian Library and found a whole new world of cafés and shops and culture to explore on my days there. Twice a week, when it was my turn to do the shared school run, I would escape from the farm for the day and have a totally different experience, all on my own. I treasured making a new routine for myself in Oxford and discovering the places I most enjoyed getting a coffee, taking a writing break, or grabbing a quick lunch. Apart from that pleasure, I also quickly realized how happy I was to see Christopher at the end of a long day when I had lots to report on and was eager to hear about the goings-on in his day as well. My days away also created a renewed sense of appreciation for the farm, and arriving home in the evenings felt romantic and calm after a day in a big town in a way that I had not felt when I was there all the time.

Through finding a better balance of being at home and being away, I also realized that it was the farm that made me feel confined as much as it was all the time I spent in such close proximity to Christopher. Both are sources of tremendous meaning and pleasure in my life, for which I am so grateful, but they were also a case of "too much of a good thing," and since I have found other sources of joy and satisfaction, I've enjoyed all of it even more.

I do thrive on the back-to-school feeling that September brings for me as well, even though in my case it's more like back-to-the-office. The time away has usually given me fresh motivation and inspiration, and I have a new appreciation for my routine that inevitably gets disrupted for most of July and August. Truth be told, though, with all that is happening in my family life and on the farm in September, it is usually October by the time I feel my balance of priorities and my work/exercise/family/house routine has gained real traction.

Regardless of the project(s) I am pursuing at any given time, working at home has its distractions—a huge difference from New York, where offices and meetings created a much more formal structure for me. It's the dream to be able to say "I work from home," but then it's up to you to create that structure. My work life these days always seems to involve some sort of writing, and whether it's a magazine article or an entire book, to be an effective writer requires a few strategies. I'm going to be very careful *not* to use the word *routine* here because my writing career distinctly lacks one, but let's just say that, in order to be productive, I have developed some habits to help me get the job done.

My Writing Habits

If you're a writer yourself, you inevitably understand how hard it can sometimes be to get your writing done. In truth, it's been many years since I moved to England, and I am still refining my work habits. The hardest thing for me has been that I don't write all the time. Because my books are always a mixture of written word and photographs, it tends to be that I write for a few weeks and then I research the illustrations for a while, and then I go back to writing. Then I finish the writing for the book and I am editing, making corrections, placing photographs in the text, and so on. It's not like writing a novel, where I would be mostly writing consistently throughout the process. Interspersed with book writing are the articles I write for magazines. So I usually have some form of writing in my life, but it's kind of all over the place. Even though I have yet to establish a regular schedule per se (who knows if I ever will?!), I have pretty much figured out how to get the work done when I need to. The following are the ways I know that let me get my writing done in and among my everyday life.

1. Wake up at seven a.m. and write for an hour. Some weeks this is all the daily writing I do, but I do it every single weekday, and I have found that I am remarkably efficient at this hour of the morning. Once the alarm goes off, I go straight to the kitchen for coffee and then take it back upstairs to my bed with my laptop. Christopher grumbles from time to time about the tapping noise of keyboard buttons while he's trying to sleep, but I love to feel cozy with my coffee in one hand and my duvet pulled up over my lap while I'm writing.

2. Go to Oxford for the day. I start the day at Turl Street Café, where they have lovely farmhouse furniture, a great latte, and a help-yourself, eat-all-you-want toast bar that is the best thing on Earth. I have one piece with butter and Marmite and another with butter and marmalade, and then sometimes go back for round two if I'm really hungry. Over breakfast, I get any nagging admin out of the way, and then I start into my writing. I work, work, work and then take a break for lunch around noon, walking around the corner to Wagamama's, where I either have pork ramen or chili chicken salad. Afterward, I walk three minutes down a narrow alleyway alongside Brasenose College to the Bodleian Library for more quiet and focused work in the afternoon. The Harry Potter–like Duke Humfrey's Library in the Bodleian was built starting in 1478 and requires a four-page application to explain why you feel you need to be there to do your writing. In my case, I made a two-page list of books they had about British countryside culture and fashion that couldn't be found elsewhere. I included my book contracts from Penguin and wrote a brief synopsis of my next book. They accepted me! Writing in the Duke Humfrey makes me take myself as seriously as possible, considering I'm writing about pretty trivial matters compared to most people working in there. I am usually surrounded by older men or studious-looking women who I assume are writing their PhD theses on some highly intellectual matter while I sit nearby writing about fashion and cooking and country life, trying to catch the vibe of their intelligence through sheer proximity. At the end of the day, it's lovely to head home to the farm and Christopher, having missed both during my day in the city (again, if you can call

Oxford a city!). Since Zach has now started at boarding school, I still go to Oxford, but less than I used to, and have added Soho Farmhouse into the mix now. It is closer to home—only a fifteen-minute drive—and I can exercise there, then write in the quiet section of the main barn and have lunch next to the roaring fire. Pretty cozy.

3. Sometimes I have no choice but to get my writing done in the middle of the day at home. This is not my first choice—too many distractions!—but I have found that either being in my office with my entire desk cleared off (and any admin out of sight) can work, or, mostly in winter, I set myself up next to the fire in the sitting room, cozy in a big armchair with a cup of tea within reach. I like to feel settled when I write—happy to be where I am and have everything I need.

4. Whenever I have a lot of writing to do or am intimidated by starting a new project, or—most commonly—have not been getting enough done at home and need to play catch-up, I take myself off on a two- or three-day writing retreat. There's the Village Pub near Bibury, one of the most beautiful and quintessentially English towns in Oxfordshire, where the rooms are reasonable, the food is good, and the chairs next to the fireplace are perfect for writing. Usually my friend Rose comes along to keep me company and my days go like this: wake up, write, breakfast with Rose, write, lunch, write, walk in the country with Rose, early supper with Rose, watch TV, bed. Or sometimes my friend Bella, who is also a writer, will host a writer's retreat at her house twenty minutes away from mine. There I'm on the same schedule and get a crazy amount of writing done. These getaways are the only times when I can write in a focused way throughout the day—away from house chores, wife/mom duty, making meals, and so on. Heaven!

Another activity we get back into after the summer—albeit slowly—is riding. After the kids are settled back into school and I have gotten a handle on balancing work and family life, Christopher and I start to ride with an eye toward the upcoming hunting season. In the November chapter, I will attempt to explain hunting and why I do it, and why I feel it's an important tradition to uphold, at least in the part of the world where we live. But for now, in September, preparation for the season involves riding more often and doing lots of long, uphill trotting to get the horses—and ourselves—fit. When we are riding often, endless trotting feels easy, but once it's been a month or two out of the saddle, it's amazing how quickly both our legs and the horses' feel depleted.

What I love most about riding in the autumn, especially in the early morning, is the fog. It arrives almost immediately after the start of September. I often wake in the morning to the dense, white cloud covering most of the countryside and I know that autumn is coming. I've never seen fog like I have seen in England. It makes me understand where the expression "blanket of fog" comes from. Being a mostly suburban and city person myself, I used to think fog was not much more than a slight nuisance for driving, but here on the farm, it captivates me. Sometimes it's so thick I actually feel scared to drive, not able to see more than a few meters in front of the car. The fog mostly comes in a thin layer, rolling up, over, and then back under the surrounding hills. When you are under it, it is all-consuming, but I love to be on the crest of a hill, over the fog, watching it like a sea of white cotton laid on the floor of the countryside. Sometimes the sun shines through, burning off the dense moisture, and the fog becomes lighter and lighter until it floats up into the sky, leaving a clear day in its wake.

*Coco practicing her hedge hopping at Antonia Davies' pre–hunting season course
in Warwickshire. I usually go to watch, but I barely can. Feels much safer to be behind
the lens of a camera not thinking too much about what she is doing.*

You'd be appalled if you knew what we ate for dinner to celebrate Zach's eleventh birthday in this cozy, country setting. Shall I tell you? KFC!!! He was having a nostalgic craving for American fried chicken, and that was the easiest way to produce it. I'm sure you think I should have made it myself, but frying oil scares me. In any case, he loved it.

And finally, at the very end of September, we celebrate Zach's birthday. Being a city kid at heart, Zach is usually most inspired to do something away from the farm to celebrate. We invite as many kids as can fit in our old Land Rover Defender (eleven total, in addition to the driver) and we head off to some exotic (at least for this part of the world) adventure, such as the Harry Potter tour at Warner Bros. Studios, a trampoline park, paintball, or laser tag—the less rural and the farther away from the farm the better! However, I did finally convince Zach to have a scavenger hunt on the farm for his thirteenth birthday. Find a chicken egg, get your picture taken with Grandma, collect some horse poop, ride a pig . . . I've been pitching this to him for years, and he finally thought it sounded like fun. The party was a huge success, easily his best ever. Does it mean that my city boy is finally becoming a farm boy? I guess there is some ambivalence on my part in considering that, because as much as I want him to be happy here, and deep down I know that he is, there's a part of me that's happy to have company in missing New York as I often do. You should see the two of us when we land in New York together—we celebrate by grabbing a Dunkin' Donut and iced coffee at the airport, jump in a Yellow Cab, and watch with our noses pressed to the window as the city unfolds before us. You can take this mom and her boy out of the city, but you can't take the city out of us!

CHAPTER V—OCTOBER

Fall in England – Autumn hunting – Pig riding – More fruit harvest
(apples, quinces, autumn raspberries) – Japanese anemones

ALTHOUGH I had spent time in England every year for fifteen years before moving here, the one season I had never witnessed was autumn. What I expected was something not so different from an American fall, but in reality it is completely different. Nature in England takes its evolution slowly and individually, with each tree turning its leaves seemingly at its own pace, whereas the American version seems to hit you over the head all at once during what is popularly known as "the peak." That glorious moment may be more spectacular, as you get the concentration of all that color at once more or less, but I enjoy the more gradual change here. Throughout October, there are areas of the farm that are still entirely green, as if summer is still lingering, while other parts might have a singular giant tree in vivid yellow with nearby hedges blanketed in bright red or orange. We also have the exposed soil of the harvest giving the land a warmer hue, only to then be replaced by the newly planted crop catching a ride on the late-season growth cycle, making all the fields bright green once again. Autumn has always been one of my favorite seasons, and I have so enjoyed the opportunity to enjoy it for longer in England, easing me more gently into the reality that soon there will be no leaves on the trees at all.

OCTOBER'S BEECHES FIRE TO THEIR FALL,
AND GOLD THE HUNTER'S MOON SHINES OVER ALL.

Another thrill of October is autumn hunting with the foxhounds. Autumn hunting is pretty much the run-up to the official season, though it's slower and gentler than the real deal, and my favorite part is that the meet (the time and place where you congregate, usually on someone's farm where there is room for plenty of horse boxes to park) is timed to sunrise. We wake in the dark, usually around four-thirty a.m., guzzle a mug of coffee (just one, otherwise I'm terrified of having to pee while out on horseback—it's one thing for men to jump off and face the hedge, a whole other thing for a girl to have to drop trou and squat), inhale two pieces of buttered toast (one with Marmite, one with marmalade), and head to the stables to load up the horses and be off by six or six-thirty a.m. As the meet changes location every week depending on where the hunting is happening, sometimes we luck out and have it at our farm or nearby. At home is obviously very civilized, but I also love hacking to the neighbors in the dark. The horses are alert and the sky is just light enough to guide the way, unless we go through

First glimpse of dawn at the Sezincote meet. Watching the sunrise
on horseback is what autumn hunting is all about for me.

a wood, which we often do, and then we are forced to rely on our horses to find their own way. Autumn hunting involves lots of waiting around while the young hounds are getting used to their new jobs. Christopher and Coco don't have much patience for this, as they'd rather be galloping around and jumping hedges, but I love sitting in a field on a horse, watching the fog clear, and, if we're lucky, the sun break through the clouds. Maybe there are thirty or forty of us in the field, and there is always someone nice to chat with or get to know for the first time—and there really is no bad view in the Cotswolds.

The other thing I love is the riding pace, which is considerably slower than in the actual hunting season. I didn't grow up riding horses, and I only learned to hunt when we moved here to live full-time. Although I am getting better and better at it, it still terrifies me. When I look back at my first season hunting, I see that I had no business at all being out there—I had no idea what I was doing and I probably put myself at great risk—

Leading my horse Shalom into the stables after a morning out. Now that I've had some time to get my outfit together I really enjoy getting dressed for hunting. I have one pair of really nice boots (handmade in Argentina and a gift from my brother-in-law), a few different hacking jackets (this one was custom-made for me by a friend in New York, Kirk Miller), a handful of britches both new and vintage, a small collection of 1930s and 40s Fair Isle vests I found on eBay, and a bunch of colored stocks. It's fun to mix and match the colors and patterns. Don't think I've ever worn the same combo twice.

but it is the only way to learn. There really is no way to prepare yourself other than increasing your confidence in cantering, galloping, and jumping all kinds of cross-country fences and hedges. To get the hang of it, you just have to get out there and do it.

Early-morning light while out autumn hunting with the Heythrop.

The first time I ever went autumn hunting was Coco's first time too. It was in October of 2012, only a few months after we had made the move to England. Christopher, having not hunted since he was a teenager and having barely even been on a horse in the intervening years, declined to join us, saying that his riding years were something from his past and were not going to be resurrected. In the fifteen years I had known him, he had never shown any interest in getting on a horse. The meet was at a nearby farm, and knowing that they would be passing through our own farm early on in the day, Caroline rang the huntsman (the man who actually oversees—"hunts"—the hounds and is the figurehead of the whole operation) to ask if we could join up with them then, which is not customary, but he agreed to it. I didn't know what to expect in any regard; I didn't even really know how hunting worked. "What are we actually going to do?" I asked Caroline. She explained the basics: how the huntsman leads the hounds from his horse, aided by the whippers-in, who help keep the hounds in line and accounted for, and then the field of followers (Coco and myself included) would be led by a field master, who gives us instructions and makes sure we allow the masters and hounds plenty of room to do their jobs. "And what do I wear?" I then asked.

It was sweet, Caroline's response. Being an Englishwoman and a traditionalist, she would have known that I had nothing in my wardrobe that came even close to being appropriate for this first day out with the hunt, so she tried her best to sound relaxed as she told me to wear whatever I had that came closest to resembling a brown or green tweed jacket and a country-ish shirt and tie, none of which I owned. The one thing I did have was proper riding boots (although not exactly in the hunting style) and a pair of cream jodhpurs, which would do just fine. From the few pieces of mostly designer clothes I had in my closet, I managed to cobble together what only just about touched on resembling hunting clothes. I had a Rag & Bone heathery green wool jacket that fortunately had the approximate shape of a hacking jacket, but unfortunately had metal military-style buttons all over it. I also dug out a Proenza Schouler black-and-white tattersall shirt—it played the part perfectly except it had a black leather patch pocket over the left breast that I prayed no one would notice once I had the jacket on over it. Coco had hairnets left over from Pony Club camp, so I borrowed one to keep my hair tidy under my hat. Coco herself was better off than me in the clothing department because she'd had to have a tweed jacket, shirt, and tie for Pony Club. She fit in much better than I did on that first day.

We set off from the stables on our horses headed to Grandma's house. I rode Polo, Coco's pony, and she took Sailor, her old pony whom she had clearly outgrown. Coco wasn't thrilled not to be on Polo, but he was the only horse I trusted for myself in a trying situation, and I knew Coco would be fine on Sailor. Both ponies had hunted their whole lives, so I knew they would keep us safe and make us look far more experienced than we were.

At the meet, Caroline introduced us to the huntsman and some of the followers, many of whom were neighbors I vaguely knew. I was nervous, knowing so little about what to expect and worried that I had gotten into something over my head. I guess I was most worried that I would embarrass Coco. Despite being an excellent and experienced rider (far better than me!), she knew as little about hunting as I did, but she was representing the Brooks family, who have hunted with the Heythrop (our local hunt) for generations and who have a reputation for being competent riders. Just before we set off, I spotted my friend Lucy, whom I know well, and she told me that she would look after Coco and me for the day. I couldn't decide if I was relieved to have someone looking after us or even more worried that someone I knew might witness the horror of my inadequacy and possible mistakes.

Coco and her hunter Jake illuminated by the rising sun at Exford Farm.

Autumn hunting often involves lots of waiting around as the young hounds learn what they are meant to be doing. Some people find it boring, but I can't complain about long stretches of staring at a view like this.

Nonetheless, off we went down our driveway and up through the pillars onto a bridle path leading to the next-door farm. We were all in a line, riding in a civilized trot through the wheat fields. Every few minutes, someone would ride up alongside us to introduce themselves, mostly people who knew Christopher from childhood Pony Club days. Everyone was exceedingly polite, friendly, and welcoming, and they seemed genuinely pleased to see us out, despite our lack of experience. My joy was immediate, as was Coco's—after years and years of hacking around our farm by myself or just with Coco, here I was in a community of people who had known the Brooks family for generations, all joining in a shared passion. Soon we were cantering around the fields with the adrenaline picking up, and then we'd stand near a wood and chat with more people who were curious to hear about

Christopher and Miranda arriving at the Sarsgrove meet in the early morning fog that is typical of autumn here.

our recent move from New York. My eyes got teary on a few occasions watching Coco ride so beautifully and her body language that showed her pride of place. We didn't stay out for long that first day—maybe an hour and a half after we set off, we passed a place from which I knew the way home. I was worried that we or the ponies might grow tired later at a place where I would not know how to get back to the farm, so we took the chance and peeled off. Back at the cottage, we collapsed on the sofa with a mix of exhaustion, relief, utter satisfaction, and joy. After hearing about our day, Christopher said, "Okay, Coco, if you're going to seriously get into this, I'm going to have to take you out and show you how it's done." And from then on, Christopher came out with us the rest of the season while we got acquainted and he got reacquainted with hunting. People couldn't believe their eyes when they saw Christopher on a horse; he had rejected that world so long ago. But he picked it up like he'd never quit, and because he *chose* to hunt now, as opposed to feeling forced to as a child, his fondness for riding and hunting is stronger than ever before. What seemed stuffy and overly traditional to Christopher as a teenager now feels like an authentic and sincere part of countryside life.

*The very first time Zach ever rode a pig,
with an assist from his uncle Charlie.*

Christopher loves to tell people how he rode ponies as a kid but that once he got on a motorcycle around age fifteen, he never rode a horse again (until recently, that is). When Zach grows up, I suspect he'll tell a similar tale, but in his case it will be pigs that lured him away from horses. When Zach was seven, his uncle Charlie got two rather large Kunekune (pronounced like CooneyCooney) pigs whom the kids rather cruelly named Porky and Bacon. Zach had had a bad fall off his pony the year before and had shied away from horse riding since, and Charlie had it in his head that Zach would find it more fun to ride the pigs! I thought it was a silly idea and didn't give it much thought until one afternoon when Charlie turned up in our garden. He was chasing the pigs, who had escaped from their yard and come to our orchard to see what they could scavenge. He called Zach out of the house and told him this was his chance to have a go. The very first time Zach sat on a pig—I'm pretty sure it was Bacon—she, quite shocked, I think, just stood there, still enough that Zach lifted his arms in the air in victory, but as he did so, the pig took off running and Zach tumbled backward straight off her back. After a pause to make sure Zach was fine, we all fell apart laughing. But by the end of that day, after a fair amount of trial and error, Zach got the hang of it, and our family pig jockey was born!

Coco has her horses, and Zach has his pigs. When guests come to visit, it's the perfect party trick—"Let's go for a walk and watch Zach ride the pigs." All of us, Zach included, end up crying with laughter.

About three years ago, the farm got three new pigs, and we were intending to breed them. The subject of the two older ones, our beloved Porky and Bacon, came up, and it was suggested they go to market to be made into sausages. Zach campaigned hard for those two pigs. Tears, acquired family allies, and some good old American emotional blackmail eventually won him his battle. They now belong to him and will live out their days in a field near our house. Ride on, Zach!

The pig riding as it evolved, with various degrees of success.

This is the youngest apple tree in our orchard, but I love it because of how red the apples are.

The explosion of fruit dies down a notch in October. The figs are nearly gone and the pears are past their prime, but there are still thousands of apples. At this point, I am fed up with preserving and baking, so instead I start making juice.

Every autumn when I was a child, my family would choose a Saturday, usually in October, to pile into the car and drive at least an hour north from our home in Westchester, New York, to pick apples and buy cider. We always returned with huge bags of tangy, crisp fruit far better than anything you could buy in the supermarket. We ate as many as we could and then my mom would make the rest into applesauce. The years of memories are hard to differentiate in my head—they have all melted together into one collection of happy fruit-picking nostalgia.

One of my favorite things about living on our farm is the ability to walk outside and pick fruit. It reminds me of my childhood summers in Florida.

When we moved to England and I found myself surrounded by more apples than one could possibly pick come autumn, the abundance quickly weighed on me. Yes, we picked them and ate them fresh off the tree, and I made a few pies or crumbles, and then as much applesauce as I could possibly make. But that didn't even scratch the surface of using most of our apple supply, and while the kids would help me pick the fruit, they would abandon the operation as soon as we got into the kitchen, neither of them being huge fans of cooking. After driving hours to appreciate the joy of apples as a child, I worried that my own children were taking the pleasure for granted.

Then last Christmas I received a juice press from my in-laws, and I hoped it would transform my guilt into a renewed feeling of efficiency. I waited for apple

*One thing both my kids love doing is making apple juice,
and I understand why—each step of the process
is both rewarding and satisfying.*

season the following October, and one Sunday Zach and I carried the press out of its storage spot in the barn to the porch of my office shed. We took a big wire basket out into the orchard and collected as much fruit as we could carry back toward the house. Then we began chopping the fruit into quarters and placing it in the crusher. The crusher is incredibly satisfying: you pile it up with chopped fruit, turn the big metal wheel, and watch the apple chunks break down as they are churned by metal cogs and then disappear into the hopper. Zach quickly decided he preferred that chore, and I was happy to continue chopping. Once the fruit piled up, we placed the round wooden top over the hopper and began to turn the press, watching it lower over the crushed fruit. Already juice was starting to stream out the bottom, and we rushed to put a pitcher in place under the spout. Zach thought it was fun to turn the pressing handle, so I managed the sudden and abundant rush of juice—quickly changing bottles (I use old wine bottles) and managing overflow. The whole process took about an hour in which both Zach and I were entirely engaged and excited. On top of that, we were left with four bottles of glorious juice.

Since then, we press juice nearly every weekend in October. Coco joins in when she comes home on the weekends and has found it equally fun and rewarding. We've experimented with all combinations of eating apples, cooking apples, and pears. My favorite juice is made from cooking apples mixed with pears—both tart and sweet. While the kids practically chug the fresh juice, I prefer it thinned out with fizzy water and a few ice cubes.

I had all sorts of plans about whom to give the fresh juice to or how to freeze it for winter, but the kids loved it so much that they drank it all by the end of the weekend. Each time we pressed juice, it would disappear as fast as we made it. It turns out that although our family apple-picking tradition is different from that of my own youth, there is no question that it is equally fun, satisfying, and memory making.

Speaking of pigs and apples, every year around this time, Porky somehow intuits (or does she smell them from so far away?) that there are apples lying on the ground in our orchard and manages to break out of her usual field to pay us frequent visits. I am usually in my office, located in close proximity to the largest apple tree in the farmyard, when I hear the first snort or catch my first glimpse of the intruder, which never fails to give me tremendous pleasure. As hard as it is to capture her and lead her back to her field, and as much havoc as she can cause when free (ripping apart full garbage bags, appearing in the house, menacing riders on the bridle path, and ravaging my sister-in-law's vegetable garden), I just love looking out my window—whether it be from my office, my bedroom, or the kitchen—and seeing Porky gorging herself on fallen apples. Sometimes I come downstairs first thing in the morning and see her in the garden right outside the window, searching for her morning snack, and I have to stop for a second to watch her and appreciate how lovely it is to wake up to a pig in my garden. This past year Porky was so good at escaping from her field and concealing the place of passage that we altogether gave up and enclosed her in a yard closer to the house where we can keep a more watchful eye on her. Poor Bacon was left back in the field all by herself for over a month.

Making apple juice is a pretty messy business, but it's satisfying to see how lovely the finished product looks at the end.

Less satisfying in our October harvest haul has been the quince. The fucking quince! We have *just one* quince tree in our farmyard, but she is a productive little tree, giving us at least a few dozen pieces of fruit each autumn. Truth be told, I had no idea what a quince even was when we first moved to England. I had heard of them, but had never eaten one and certainly couldn't have identified one if asked. So the first year I was here, I was optimistic and ambitious and thought—inspired by my friend Kevin West's book *Saving the Season*—I would make Quince Jelly (see page 162 for recipe) and then use the leftover pulp to make *membrillo*, a quince paste that is excellent served with cheese and makes a nice hostess gift when wrapped in waxed paper and tied up with twine. Well, I was immediately frustrated by the jelly. I couldn't use my proper copper preserving pan because at the time I had an induction stove (which doesn't work with copper pans), so I used a Le Creuset Dutch oven and the sugar slightly burned. Buzzkill. Soldiering on, I attempted the quince paste, which requires an ambitious amount of cooking time (or drying out, shall we say), and I was unsure of myself throughout the whole process. But it was perfect! I wrapped them up, just as I had imagined, and gave them to friends as presents in the following weeks. It must have been beginner's luck, because I've never had success with the *membrillo* since, always

This quince paste scenario (wrapped in wax paper and twine) looks so civilized—but if you only knew the work and occasional frustration that go into making it!

burning it or drying it out too much. I have had a degree of better luck with the jelly, but I found that even when I made it as close to correctly as I could expect of myself, I ended up giving most of it away to my mother-in-law. After it turned out well enough, I wondered what the hell to do with Quince Jelly anyway. I solved one problem when I posed this question to my friend Claire Ptak, who runs Violet bakery, my favorite, in London. Her toastie recipe has rendered me slightly less generous in giving away much of my Quince Jelly.

The third time I found myself in quince season, I decided to make the jelly, skip the paste, and also try something new: roasted quince. Well, the quince gods weren't shining on me then, either, because I got distracted and burned them to a crisp, which is so not like me! I was furious, and so demoralized that I let the rest of them rot on the ground. Childish, I know.

In the end, I am pretty sure my quince tree is cursed, because this past year I handed the whole operation to my poor house guest, Emilie, and she had equally bad luck. We thought we'd make a big Sunday lunch for whoever was on the farm that weekend. Shying away from my quince performance anxiety, I handed her a Nigel Slater recipe for caramelized roasted quince (which we planned to serve with vanilla ice cream for dessert), pointed to where to find the fruit stored in the barn, and let her have at it while I made Chicken Potpies from scratch. Poor, poor Emilie. Turns out my

I often enlist Coco to help me pick fruit, as she is two inches taller than I am. This is especially true with the quince, as there aren't that many, so each one is precious and must be harvested. The quince are also inconsistent in their abundance. Some years we'll get three dozen perfect fruits and others just a handful of small ones. Doesn't seem to be any rhyme or reason.

Chicken Potpies (see page 235 for recipe)—served individually in adorable miniature Le Creuset cocottes—were my best ever. They were a big success. But sadly the quince dessert was *awful*. The quinces were undercooked, they didn't caramelize, and they even looked ugly. Despite Emilie's embarrassment, I was secretly thrilled it wasn't only me with the quince disasters. It's possible I just haven't found the right recipe for quinces yet, and when I do, all of these troubles will melt away. For some reason, I'm compelled to keep trying. Maybe because there is just that one tree of perfect-looking quinces? Or maybe it's because I've done so well with the apples, pears, plums, figs, and berries that I can't bear failing with this frustrating fruit? Whatever it is, there is always another season to try again.

QUINCE JELLY
Adapted from Kevin West's *Saving the Season*

YIELDS ABOUT FOUR 8-OUNCE JARS

5 pounds quinces
10 cups water

4 cups granulated sugar
2 tablespoons freshly squeezed lemon juice

Quarter the quinces, removing the stems and calyx (flower remnant) but leaving the peels and cores. Slice each quarter into smaller chunks. Place in a large pot and add the water to barely cover.

Bring to a boil, then lower the heat and simmer for $1\frac{1}{2}$ hours, partially covered, until the quinces are very soft and slightly pink.

Strain the quinces through a damp jelly bag or a colander lined with damp cheesecloth and catch the pectin stock in a bowl. Allow to drop for 30 minutes. You should have about 4 cups of pectin stock.

Spread the sugar on a baking sheet, and warm it in an oven set to 225°F for 15 minutes. Combine the pectin stock, sugar, and lemon juice in a preserving pan. Reduce over high heat to the gel point, 20 minutes or more, then turn off the heat. Skim the jelly and ladle into four prepared 8-ounce jars, leaving a $\frac{1}{4}$-inch headspace. Seal, and let the jars sit in a boiling-water bath for 10 minutes.

CHEDDAR AND SCALLION TOASTIE WITH QUINCE JELLY
Adapted from Claire Ptak's *The Violet Bakery Cookbook*

When people recommend I eat a certain jam or jelly with cheese, that immediately makes me crave it as a complement to my childhood favorite sandwich, a grilled cheese. Like Fig Jam, I find that Quince Jelly is best eaten between two layers of buttery toast and a thick layer of well-paired cheese.

sourdough bread
salted butter
mature Cheddar cheese, grated
scallions, thinly sliced

sea salt and black pepper
Quince Jelly (page 162)
cornichons, for serving (optional)

Slice the sourdough bread very thinly and spread one slice with butter. Add a scoop of grated Cheddar cheese and scatter with a few thin slices of scallions. Season with salt and pepper and top with a second slice of bread.

Heat a heavy-bottomed frying pan or a skillet. Melt a little butter in it and add the sandwich. Resist the temptation to press too hard, or all the cheese will come out of the sides. Toast until the bread is golden brown and the cheese is melted. Serve on a plate with a small bowl of Quince Jelly for dipping. This is also good with a few cornichons.

On a more successful note, one of the most thrilling additions to our October garden came about completely by accident. In one of our early springs spent in England, Christopher made the very sweet and romantic decision to plant an entire hedge of raspberry bushes in the orchard as a Mother's Day present to me. He planted them out all beautifully in a row, supported by wooden stakes and wire. The whole thing looked immaculate, but the following spring, nothing happened . . . no fruit. It was such a disappointment. In October of that year, however, we walked into the orchard one day and my beautiful bushes were bursting with raspberries! By accident, Christopher had planted autumn raspberries . . . but what a fantastic surprise. As we have summer raspberries in another area of our garden, we now have two glorious crops of one of my favorite fruits, and the late version couldn't be better timed—just when you think the fruit season is over, you get a whole new supply that lasts well into November. A few years into our new crop, the plants are so prolific that we can't possibly eat them all, and so I take pleasure in first cooking them into something more hearty like Raspberry Corn Muffins (see page 165) for autumn breakfasts, and eventually freezing any we don't eat immediately to save for winter, when summer fruit seems so far away.

The optimistic, summery vibe of autumn raspberries.

RASPBERRY CORN MUFFINS

MAKES 12 MUFFINS

1 cup yellow cornmeal
1 cup all-purpose flour
$^1/_2$ cup granulated sugar
1 teaspoon baking powder
1 teaspoon baking soda

$^1/_4$ teaspoon sea salt
2 large eggs
1$^1/_4$ cups plain yogurt
$^1/_2$ stick unsalted butter, melted and cooled
1 cup fresh raspberries

Preheat the oven to 375°F and generously butter a twelve $^1/_2$-cup muffin pan.

In a bowl, whisk together the cornmeal, flour, sugar, baking powder, baking soda, and salt.

In another bowl, whisk together the eggs, yogurt, and butter, add the flour mixture, and stir the batter until it is just combined. Gently fold in the raspberries, divide the batter among the muffin cups, and bake in the middle of the oven for 20 minutes, or until a tester comes out clean.

Let the muffins cool in the pan on a wire rack for 3 minutes, turn them out onto the rack, and let them cool completely.

As with the autumn raspberries, I am also grateful for the Japanese anemones in the flower beds in October. Elsewhere in the garden we do have some late-blooming roses, and the hollyhocks are usually still around against the back of the house, but in the main garden, just when the vast majority of the flowers have come and gone, the front beds fill with those feminine and delicate lavender flowers that make us feel like we're right back in the lushest part of the year. Truth be told, they have self-seeded so much that we probably have too many of them, but I am loath to cut them back. The abundance gives me a guilt-free excuse to pick them liberally and gather into a vase for the house or to give to friends—I can't describe how lovely it feels to show up for a Sunday lunch in October with an armful of fresh-picked flowers for our hostess.

The lush display of Japanese anemones, the last (but not least!) flower to bloom in the garden beds.

CHAPTER VI—NOVEMBER

Combating the gloom – Start of the hunting season – Knitting –
Cooking heartier, cozier food – Thanksgiving traditions

NOVEMBER is the time of year when I really start to keep my eye on the weather. The days are nearly at their shortest, and they are often filled with clouds and fog. I know it sounds gloomy, but here's the thing about the dreaded English weather: yes, it can at times be horrible and demoralizing, but on the whole, it's not *that* bad. Really. I have just had to get the hang of it, which mostly entails dropping everything, no matter how important, to run outside when the sun is shining. As long as I get my hour or so of outdoor time each day, or even just most days, I am fine. Take a recent Friday, for example. The kids were home on their half-term break, so I planned to ride with them in the morning when the sun was even just hinting at coming out. But they were not having it—they were dead set on having a lazy morning. And then the rain started, and it poured for most of the day. By late afternoon, we were all having a bit of cabin fever, so I finally persuaded them to ride. Although it was forecast to rain into the evening, the sun broke through the clouds, and, much to our surprise, it became the perfect autumn day. We closed our eyes as we sat on our horses and turned our faces toward the sun.

NOVEMBER'S SUN, A GREAT SKY-APPLE OF GOD,
HANGS LOW AND RED ABOVE THE NEW-TURNED SOD.

We let the warmth and the glow of light sink into our skin. We talked about how good it felt and savored the moment. As we turned toward home, a big dark cloud threatened to disturb our bliss, but the rain just missed us, and instead we were treated to a giant double rainbow right over the pillars that mark the old entrance to the farm. We were all silent for a moment, not finding the words to express our wonder. It rained for the next day and a half, but having had our little dose of vitamin D, we were quite happy to sit inside by the fire all cozy with our magazines, card games, and laptops. Then a few days later, just as I sat down to catch up on ten days of ignored paperwork and e-mails, the sun appeared again and Ginger whined outside my office door, as if to say, "Come on, Mommy, let's go catch the sun!" I knew better than to ignore this invitation, tempting as it was to put my head down and get work done. So off we went. And that's how it works. Sometimes I luck out, and other times I have to be willing to change plans on a whim.

But no matter the circumstances, if I make the sun my priority, everything else the English weather system throws my way seems just about bearable. Knowing that the days are getting shorter and the leaves are quickly disappearing, I try to

Gingy surveying her territory. I never stop feeling happy for her—that she was rescued from dire circumstances in South Carolina and now lives a pretty ideal dog's life far away in England.

Horseback selfie with rainbow.

walk Ginger more than I normally would, just to savor the end of the season and store up some beauty and sunshine for the long winter months that lie ahead.

In addition to getting me out and about on the farm, November is also the month that marks the beginning of the official hunting season, offering abundant opportunities for excitement, adrenaline, exercise, fresh air, and all the wild weather the season has to offer. My first-ever glimpse of the hunt was long before we had moved here, while we were visiting family, and it happened right outside my bedroom window in the very early hours of the morning.

Christopher shook me awake, saying, "The hounds! I hear the hounds!" I looked at the clock—five-thirty a.m.—and then at him with an expression that conveyed I had no idea what he was talking about. "Quick! Run to the window!" he insisted. So I pulled the curtains aside and stuck my head out the open window. There were two immaculate gentlemen wearing hunter green wool coats and black velvet hats,

You'd be surprised how many women still choose to ride sidesaddle around where we live, whether it be out hunting or joining in a race at the local point-to-point. Their outfit, known as a habit, gives me a thrill and I am particularly enthralled when, like this lass above, they wear a veil under their bowler hat. So chic.

trotting on horses with a sea of hounds following them, and then another two identical-looking men riding at the back of the pack. The whole thing looked like a Bruce Weber photograph for a Ralph Lauren ad, except that it was *real*. I was mesmerized, having never seen anything like it. But they were gone in a flash, and I was left with just that fleeting moment in my mind.

A few years later, we spent a Christmas in England and took baby Coco to the Boxing Day meet in Chipping Norton. It's a real community event, the whole town turns up for it, and it's festive and lively. People in a farming community such as ours are proud of our hunt, whether they follow it or not. This time I got a better sense of the hunting scene—the masters, the huntsman, the field—even though I still wasn't entirely clear how it all worked and what it was exactly that they did. But again, I was intrigued. If you're from anywhere outside of England, seeing the hunt for the first time is like getting trapped in a time warp, especially seeing the handful of men in top hats and tails and the women in veils and habits—that's not the norm anymore, but I still get excited when I see the odd person throwing it back to the old-school days. Even so, no one looks bad in even the newest of riding clothes—it's a uniform that just works. So my first attraction to the hunt had more to do with style and romance than it did with participation, aside from wanting to wear all the clothes I saw.

This is the boot room scene in the home of most hunting families. All the kit—coats, boots, hats, and whips—are immaculately cleaned after each day out and hung tidily, waiting for their next adventure.

Since moving to England, and having my first few days out (actually mounted!) with the hunt during the early days of the season in September and October, I have slowly put one foot in front of the other and gotten more and more involved each season.

Here's how it works: four times a week the hunt "meets" on someone's land within the catchment area of the hunt. Our hunt is called the Heythrop, and it covers much of the Oxfordshire and Gloucestershire countryside. Fairgreen Farm is pretty much in the middle of the Heythrop country, and we usually host the meet ourselves once or twice a year. Hosting the meet includes providing space for everyone to park their trailers and lorries, to mount their horses, and to gather all in one area where the "field" of masters and followers, both on foot and on horse, are served food and drink—typically some sort of sausage roll and a glass of port. On days like Saturdays or holidays when lots of children are out, they also pass around baskets of chocolates, and I always line my pockets! It's amazing how hungry I get out hunting no matter how much I've had for breakfast and managed to scarf down at the meet. After a welcome speech from the huntsman (the man who leads the hounds and masters), he sets off across the countryside

followed by his pack of hounds and a handful of various other masters in supporting professional roles such as the whipper-in, who keeps any misbehaving hounds in line and supports leading them in the right direction. The huntsman will head from cover to cover in search of a pre-laid trail. These days, since hunting actual foxes has been made illegal, a simulated scent has been dragged along a predetermined route in advance. The field of mounted followers is led by the field master, and he makes sure we are as close as possible to the actual "hunting" without disturbing the huntsman and hounds in action. For example, you never ride off in front of the field master, and you never, ever, get in front of the huntsman.

Matt, a member of the Heythrop, is always the most immaculately turned out for hunting: top hat, tails, and all.

The Heythrop huntsman and his hounds at the Fifield meet.

I hunt on Polo (a lifelong veteran and the most reliably safe horse to ride on our farm) as much as possible, although now he's too old to be taken out more than just occasionally. This picture was taken right after we arrived home on the last day of Polo's final full season out hunting. He looks so exhausted. This is when I knew it was time for him to semi-retire, age twenty-three.

The meet usually commences at 10:45 a.m., and hunting continues until dark. In between those hours, you walk, trot, canter, and even gallop across the countryside, often jumping fences, walls, and hedges to avoid slowing down by having to pass through a gate. Many people call it a day at "second horses" around two-thirty or three p.m., when you have the option of giving your first horse a rest and switching to your second horse. Christopher occasionally rides a second horse, but I never do, always too exhausted from a combination of nerves and fatigue to even consider it.

The more I see and do, the more compelled I am to continue. People say that hunting is elitist, but I have yet to see a social activity that brings a more diverse group of country folks together, whether on horse or on foot. In England, every kind of person in the countryside gets involved with the hunt whether he be riding a horse or driving an ATV, following the field up close or from afar, drinking port or closing gates. With so many affluent Londoners descending on the Cotswolds and all the attendant gentrification—pubs becoming more sophisticated, larger houses being built, and schools becoming more competitive—the hunt, as traditional as it is, stands out as something that is authentic and sincere. As a foreign newcomer, albeit one who married into a well-established local hunting family, I have been generously welcomed and included—well, except for one snooty woman who once yelled at me for riding on someone's grass; she had a point, even though it was a humbling way to learn the lesson. I've had a million other things to learn as well: follow the field master; don't ride on the crops; don't get too close to a horse with a red ribbon around his tail (it kicks!); stay at the back of the pack if you don't want to jump hedges; profusely thank anyone who stops their car for you, opens a gate, or points you in the direction of the field when lost; the older and more worn your clothes and boots are the cooler; et cetera, et cetera, et cetera.

On the actual riding front, I still have a lot to learn as well. The first season I went out with the Heythrop, I was confident for the most part as a rider, but I had never jumped at all, so when faced with a fence, wall, or hedge, I would follow the mothers and children and assorted oldies to find a gate to pass through. This meant I would become separated from Coco and Christopher, who jump everything in sight, and it would often take up to an hour or so before I found them again. Although it was a good way to get to know people, I often felt lonely on my own, or a burden if I made Christopher come with me, so I ended the first season determined to learn how to jump during the following summer months.

The other challenge I had was to get in better physical shape for hunting—I had barely made it out for longer than two hours that first season, overwhelmed by adrenaline and physical exhaustion—and I knew it was a pain for Christopher when I asked him to take me home long before he was ready to call it a day.

So by opening meet the following year, I had had some lessons, done a hunting training course (lots of very scary hedge hopping!), and done plenty of riding leading up to the season. I had the confidence that I could jump if I had to, but not so much that I particularly wanted to. It's a long way from jumping in a school or even on a cross-country course with just a handful of horses and riders, to jumping in a pack of fifty to a hundred horses all excited, with their blood up and ready to go. But still, it helped. I made it out for longer stretches, although I still couldn't keep up with Christopher's stamina, and since Coco was at boarding school, it wasn't quite as much fun for me. Christopher was getting more and more serious about his hunting, and his talent and drive were just leagues ahead of mine. He was leaving me in the dust, training to improve his skills on the days he wasn't hunting, while I was too busy writing or traveling to join in with him. At the end of that second season, I kind of felt that the novelty had worn off, and it was too much effort and time for me to invest in as a "leisure" activity.

To my surprise, though, something keeps bringing me back to hunting each season. I don't make it out for too many days, but when I get a craving to do it, I go! Despite my fledgling ability, I simply love riding, and hunting is a great way to spend the better part of a day doing that while also enjoying nature, seeing friends, and getting a bit of a thrill. And slowly, slowly, slowly, every time I do

*Autumn in the orchard. The wood-burning hot tub comes in handy after a long day
of activity, whether it be working in the garden or riding a horse.*

ride and I do jump, I get braver and stronger. This past year I made it to second
horses for the first time. I have no ambition to commit to a second horse myself, but Christopher was so proud of me for finally finishing the day when most
other people do. Also, my jumping is evolving. While I attempt only the smallest
of hedges, I jump most other stone walls and post-and-rail fences when it's obviously the most efficient way to go. If I'm at all tired or daunted and there is a gate
next to a jump, however, I will usually go through it rather than risk an accident.

Along with my increasing confidence as a rider, I am also becoming more aware
on a personal level of why people who live in the country like to hunt as an activity. We crave it as a means to get through the short days of the dark and gloomy
winter. We need a reason to wake in the morning filled with nerves and end the
day filled with exhaustion and relief. Also, it's a skill to work at, to constantly improve upon. I don't know if I will ever call myself a die-hard hunting devotee, but
I have come to appreciate it as an essential part of country life.

If hunting brings excitement and action to the winter season, the activity to balance out the adrenaline is knitting. Yes, I have become that much of a country
cliché! My knitting circle is a motley crew of city and country women of all ages.
We knit in a neighbor's barn with a giant disco ball above our heads! We knit in

the early hours of the evening, learning new stitches and techniques, supported by two knitting teachers who take the train down from London. Once we have made enough progress and drunk enough red wine, we chat and eat and even dance. Once a friend's musician husband decided to DJ the knitting night, and I didn't get home till two in the morning. The result of knitting night, despite an excellent dose of fun, was that I discovered the meditative quality of making a scarf, which is all I've ever known how to do. Yes, my stitch and my yarn have evolved—I've worked my way up to cashmere!—but mostly I just enjoy having something to do with my hands while watching TV or sitting in front of the fire, and my ambition doesn't reach much beyond that.

With the last few white autumn roses fading away on the facade of the cottage, the growing season comes to an end and I turn my energy toward activities inside the house. Planning and cooking meals is probably my favorite activity in the colder months, with my attention turning toward heartier, cozier food. We are big fans of roast meat in our house, except for Coco, who is a pescatarian, so I like to challenge myself to make satisfying meatless meals. Kedgeree is a big hit in that regard—a rice dish that can be easily improvised based on ingredients you have on hand. It works well for lunch or dinner, and even reheated for breakfast as many Brits do. I have tried many variations and can even pull off my own take on it without a recipe, but I always come back to my very favorite version, which I picked up at the fish counter at Tesco! Another meat-free meal that works at any time of day is roasted vegetables with two fried eggs on top, a simple formula based on what I have around.

Autumn crocuses under the treehouse. Another lovely result
of Christopher's bulb-planting obsession.

SMOKED HADDOCK AND LEEK KEDGEREE

Kedgeree is a traditional Scottish (by way of India) dish and is one of my favorite anytime-of-the-day meals.

SERVES 4

10 ounces smoked haddock
3 eggs, in shell for boiling
2 ounces unsalted butter, plus extra
    to butter the dish
1 large leek, trimmed and sliced
1 teaspoon mild curry powder

5 ounces basmati rice
7 ounces baby spinach
zest and juice of 2 unwaxed lemons, plus 1
    lemon for serving
handful of chives, chopped
sea salt and black pepper

Preheat the oven to 350°F. Place the haddock in a buttered baking dish and cover with foil. Bake for 10 to 12 minutes, until the fish just flakes easily. Flake into large pieces in the dish, re-cover, and set aside.

Place the eggs in a pan of boiling water and simmer for 9 minutes. Cool under cold water, crack the shells to let the air out, and set aside.

Heat half the butter in a saucepan over low heat. Add the leek and cook for 5 minutes. Add the curry powder and cook for 2 minutes more.

Stir the rice into the saucepan with a pinch of salt. Pour in 1 2/3 cups water, bring to a boil, and reduce heat to a simmer. Cover the pan and cook for 12 minutes, or until all the water has been absorbed. Remove from heat and stir in the spinach. Cover and leave to wilt for 2 minutes.

Peel and quarter the eggs. Carefully fold in the flaked haddock, the finely grated zest and juice of 1 lemon, the remaining butter, two-thirds of the chives, and salt and pepper to taste. Spoon into a serving dish and arrange the eggs on top with the remaining chives. Place the remaining lemon, cut into wedges, on the side.

Cauliflower Cheese

Adapted from Tamasin Day-Lewis's *Tamasin's Kitchen Bible*

The great thing about Cauliflower Cheese is that it works equally well as a side dish with roast meat or on its own as a cozy, comforting meal for cheese lovers and vegetarians alike. On its own I just serve it with a salad mixed with a quite tart dressing to cut the richness.

SERVES 4–6

Béchamel Sauce:

1 ¹/₂ pints milk
1 bay leaf
1 medium onion, peeled and stuck with
*   a couple of cloves*
2 ounces salted butter
1 heaping tablespoon all-purpose flour
grated nutmeg
sea salt and black pepper

Cauliflower Cheese:

1 large organic cauliflower,
*   broken into florets*
1 tablespoon grain mustard or 1 teaspoon
*   English mustard powder*
3–4 ounces mature farmhouse
*   Cheddar, grated*
1 tablespoon cream (optional)
2 ounces fresh Parmesan cheese, grated

Béchamel Sauce:

Place the milk, bay leaf, and onion in a small saucepan. Set the pan over medium-high heat and slowly bring the milk to a boil. Turn off the heat. Cover and allow to infuse for 20–30 minutes.

Melt the butter over low heat in a small, heavy-bottomed pan. Just as the butter begins to foam and bubble, throw in the flour and stir gently for a few seconds. Too much flour, and you'll get a thick floury base layer in the pan instead of a thin, bubbling one; too little, and the butter won't amalgamate with the flour, so scatter in a little more if this is the case. Let this bubble together for a minute or so, until it begins to turn a pale biscuit color, but don't let it darken and begin to burn. Reheat the onion milk over medium-high heat. The mixture will bubble furiously; whisk it furiously with a small balloon whisk until it suddenly thickens beyond easy whisking. Add 1/2 cup of the onion milk to the roux. Add more milk and repeat; the sauce will take a little longer to thicken each time you add more milk.

Let the sauce cook slowly, stirring constantly with a wooden spoon—you should have whisked out the lumps by now—and add more milk if necessary. Cook for 20 minutes, remembering to stir frequently to prevent it sticking to the bottom of the pan and burning, which milk has a tendency to do, and to prevent a skin forming on the surface.

Sprinkle the nutmeg into the sauce about halfway through the cooking time and season it with salt and pepper. When it is cooked, check the seasoning again and adjust if necessary. Reduce heat to low.

Cauliflower Cheese:

While the béchamel is cooking, bring a large pan of salted water to a boil. Add the cauliflower and cook for about 5 minutes or until the stalks have just barely softened. A fork will tell you all you need to know. Drain in a colander.

While the cauliflower is cooking, finish the sauce. Stir mustard into the béchamel and begin to add the Cheddar cheese. When you have the strength of flavor you like, stop. Adjust the seasoning or mustard if you need to and add a little cream if you feel like it, no more than a tablespoon or two.

Place the cauliflower in a gratin dish and pour an unctuous cloak of the béchamel to cover. Scatter a good handful of Parmesan over the top and either put it under the grill or in a hot oven until you've got a lovely dark mahogany pattern on top and the sauce is bubbling.

Fried Eggs over Roasted Vegetables

This favorite autumn meal was inspired by a breakfast I once had at Keith McNally's Morandi in New York City. I don't remember the exact ingredients of Keith's version, but each time I make my own by keeping this basic combination of ingredients in my head.

Serves 1

*any root vegetable (potato, sweet potato,
    parsnip, Jerusalem artichokes), diced*
olive oil
sea salt and black pepper
1 medium onion, chopped
chickpeas, strained

2 cloves minced garlic
*3 handfuls any leafy green (Swiss chard,
    spinach, Tuscan kale), coarsely chopped*
2 eggs
Parmesan, grated

Preheat the oven to 400°F. Toss the root vegetable with some olive oil, salt and pepper and roast for 20 minutes until soft and brown.

Meanwhile, in a frying pan, sauté the onion on medium-high for 3 minutes and then add the chickpeas. Keep the heat up while allowing the excess liquid from the chickpeas to evaporate. I like to let both the onions and the chickpeas get a little brown and crispy.

In another frying pan, sauté the garlic in a little oil and then add the leafy greens and cook until tender and wilted. Add the greens to the chickpea-onion mixture and use the same pan to fry the eggs to your liking.

When everything is ready, scoop a big spoonful of the roasted root vegetables onto your plate, top with the onions, chickpeas, and leafy greens, and then place the fried eggs on top. Season with salt and pepper to taste and sprinkle with Parmesan.

Coco out for an autumn hack on Shalom.

November also brings with it the excitement of Thanksgiving. Yes, even in England—well, actually, *especially* in England—we celebrate our American traditions with pride. As a Yankee myself, I am very purist about what we serve and eat, whether it's at my house, my in-laws', or at our American neighbors'. I don't want to see any typically English roast potatoes or Bread Sauce on the table. We can save that deliciousness for Christmas, when I am happy to embrace local tradition. But Thanksgiving for me—and every American has their own personal preferences—is about roast turkey with stuffing and gravy, both mashed potatoes and sweet potato casserole (*avec* marshmallows), peas, creamed onions, and cranberry sauce from a jar. I do have to apologize about the jar. Growing up, my mother prided herself on her homemade cranberry sauce with grated orange peel, but my sister and I sadly never evolved much past the Ocean Spray version in a can. Now in England I am happy to accept the organic version in a jar from our nearby farmshop, but the closer it tastes to the kid version from the supermarket, the more I am going to like it. And then of course there are the pies, and I prioritize my favorite two: pumpkin and pecan.

What I love about Thanksgiving in England is that it feels like our own private holiday, requiring me to get special permission to bring the kids home from school to celebrate our American tradition as a family. However, I have realized over the last few years that like many American holidays, such as Halloween and Valentine's Day, Thanksgiving is increasing in popularity in England, with so many ex-pats sharing our custom of gratitude and celebration with English friends and family. I have learned the hard way that to get everything I want for my English Thanksgiving, I have to plan early—these days the local shops sell out of key items like turkey and pecans as the fourth Thursday in November draws near. Besides the cooking, our hallmark Thanksgiving traditions include saying grace while all holding hands around the table (this always causes at least a little frisson of excitement for everyone . . . I once witnessed my mother's husband and ex-husband holding hands!), and taking turns going around the table making everyone say what we are grateful for. We all get shy and embarrassed and my husband teases me for being cheesy, but the result is always a great mixture of sincerity, generosity, and irreverence—too valuable to cast aside no matter where we celebrate the holiday. What reassures me is that my gratitude, Christopher's, Coco's, and yes, even Zach's mostly centers on our life here at the farm. Coco is grateful for all the animals she gets to live with, Zach is grateful for his "freedom," Christopher is grateful that I am willing to live on the farm with him, and I am grateful that our bold and scary move—that I instigated—has given me the chance to watch my whole family thrive in ways I couldn't imagine back in New York City. Long may it last!

CHAPTER VII—DECEMBER

Hard frost – Difficult decisions about horses – Christmas on the farm

I'LL never forget the first time I woke up to a hard frost on the farm. It was the first week in December, and I was up early to collect my mother from the airport. It was her first time visiting since we'd moved to England, and I was really hoping for some good weather while she was here. The day before her arrival was the foggiest one I'd seen. Even the heaviest fog in the morning usually clears by the afternoon, but this fog remained like a blanket over the countryside for the entire day. It was so dense that I had been nervous on the drive to pick up the kids from school that evening, and I was even more nervous that if it didn't lift, I would have to drive all the way to the Birmingham Airport the following

EAGER WITH FROST EACH BRIGHT DECEMBER STAR,
AND THAT OF BETHLEHEM THE BRIGHTEST FAR.

morning with terrible visibility. So I opened the curtains when I woke up and was delighted to see that the sun was shining. In fact, it looked like we'd gotten a light dusting of snow in the night. After my coffee and toast, I left the house and headed toward the car. I was looking at the "snow" and realizing it wasn't exactly snow. It was white, and it covered everything, but it sparkled as if sprayed with glitter. Every vein on every leaf and every branch on every tree was delicately and immaculately outlined in white. Before setting off, I stuck my head back in the front door and called up to Christopher to look out the window. Instead he came downstairs and walked outside with me. "Oh, it's a hard frost. It happens when there is a lot of moisture in the fog that freezes," he explained. I couldn't believe how beautiful it was. With a few minutes to spare, I ran back inside and grabbed my camera and walked up to the pillars that mark one side of the property and then around the farmyard. I had never seen anything like it, and I walked around in wonder, snapping away. Even better, I got to share this extreme beauty with my mother later in the day. The way Christopher talked about it, like it was a normal occurrence, made me think I'd see this phenomenon regularly in the winter. Well, I have seen a more moderate hard frost or two since that first time, but I have never seen anything as stunning or dramatic in the winters since.

Top: A frost-covered spider's web on the herb garden boxwood. Bottom: A wall creeper in the farmyard perfectly outlined in frozen fog.

An unusually wintry view of the driveway leading up to our house.

Coco's final good-bye with Murphy. Heartbreaking.

Early winter has often been a time when we are forced to make hard decisions about horses. When Coco was just five, we made the horribly difficult decision to put down Mr. Teddy, her first and all-time most-beloved horse. He might have been the oldest pony ever (some estimates put him in his forties) and he had really struggled to get through the past few winters. We were in New York at the time, and my mother-in-law rang Christopher to say she felt it was cruel to put him through another long stretch of living outdoors in the cold, destined to lose weight and be further weakened by the harsh conditions. My heart broke when I had to tell Coco that Mr. Teddy was gone.

The second time we decided to put a horse down was the first winter after we moved here. This time it was Murphy, and it was equally heartbreaking. Here's the thing: the real heart and soul of our farm is the horses. We live among these beautiful, oversize, prehistoric creatures. We love them, we fear them, we revere them. They live for many decades (often three or more), far longer than the other pets. Murphy was easily thirty when we began to question whether his life had run its course. He had been losing teeth for years. Each year we would debate whether he would live another winter, and he always did. But the stakes got higher and higher as he got thinner and more frail. He could no longer eat the hard food that the other horses enjoyed in the winter. We'd have to soak his meal for an hour so that he could slurp it up. And even then he couldn't get it all in. His belly would swell from the lack of proper digestion, but his hips and shoulders were emaciated. When all the other horses trotted across the field, he shuffled slowly, as if in pain. We just couldn't imagine him losing any more weight—as he inevitably would in the coming winter.

Murphy had been my niece's horse for a time, and she quickly outgrew him; then I rode him, and then my little sister rode him, and then our houseguests and friends rode him. He was a fixture on the farm, as was Mr. Teddy before him, and as oldies Polo and Sailor are now. They serve us well, and we keep them around long after their prime has come and gone. Each time I drive by them in the field, I roll down my window and say hello. They really are our family here.

In the case of Murphy, Christopher and I had never seen a horse put down, and we felt compelled to watch. We both wanted to understand what we were consenting to, should we be in a position to make more of these decisions in the future. After a weekend of painful but loving good-byes with the children, we stood in the stable-yard holding hands, with Ginger sitting beside us, preparing ourselves to see Murphy leave

Murphy's moment of late-in-life glory on the cover of J.Crew (ridden by Coco, left).

this world. When the shot rang out, it was horrible. Really, truly horrible. Ginger flinched at the violent noise and moved closer to me. But it was over instantly, and there was no question that Murphy felt nothing. I managed not to cry in front of the groom and the man from the hunt who would take him away. In our part of the world, any dead farm animals are donated to feed the local foxhounds. Afterward, I took Ginger for a walk and let the tears flow.

Later in the day, I dug up pictures of all of us with Murphy throughout his life. His superstar moment was surely when he was featured on the cover of the J.Crew catalog in 2013. I showed all the photos to the kids at dinner that night. They had cried on and off for three days, knowing that the end was coming, but there was this one picture of Murphy trotting across a field, maybe seven or eight years earlier. Coco couldn't believe that it was him. His happy, healthy self was completely unrecognizable to her. That's when I knew we'd done the right thing.

Moving on from the sadness, which is difficult to share but is an essential part of farm life, once we are past the first week in December, the rest of the month pretty much revolves around Christmas.

In the early part of the month, I am focused on sending cards, buying gifts, and assembling my annual *Life on the Farm* book, which is a collection of my photos to document all that has happened on the farm from an animal and nature perspective. I give it as a Christmas gift to every member of the Brooks family who live or have lived on the farm in years past. I also get busy making batch after batch of my favorite jam—Chili and Red Pepper—to give as presents to the kids' schoolteachers and keep enough to fulfill our own needs for the winter. Having preserved all that the farm itself has to offer in the earlier part of the autumn, my jam-making obsession is not quite satisfied until this is complete. As we don't have wind tunnels on the farm, I can't grow chilis and peppers myself, so rather unromantically I buy the ingredients from the grocery store. I learned from my friend Trinny shortly after I moved here that the idea of buying fruit in order to preserve it is decidedly un-English and even considered indulgent, but in this case I love the sweet and spicy combo of these flavors so much that I am willing to take any resulting criticism.

The living room of the cottage on Christmas morning the first time
I woke up before the children did. It was very quiet!

CHILI AND RED PEPPER JAM
Adapted from Diana Henry's *Salt Sugar Smoke*

I first fell in love with chili jam when it was served at a friend's house alongside filet mignon and potatoes dauphinoise. When I first started preserving, I bought Diana Henry's *Salt Sugar Smoke* to guide me along and felt inspired to try her version of it for myself. I have found that the jam is like Tabasco, and once you decide you like the flavor, you want to eat it on almost anything! I particularly like it with Indian food, any roast meat, kedgeree, and spread over a strong hard cheese, like Cheddar.

FILLS EIGHT 8-OUNCE JARS

8 red peppers, halved, deseeded, and chopped
8 medium-size red chilis, halved and chopped with their seeds

2 pounds, 12 ounces granulated sugar
1 pint white wine vinegar
$^1/_2$ pint liquid pectin

Put all ingredients, except pectin, into a large saucepan. Bring to a boil, then reduce heat and simmer until vegetables are really tender.

Bring the mixture to a boil, add the pectin, stir, and return to a boil. Test for the setting point. Skim any scum off the surface, ladle into warm, dry, sterilized jars, cover with waxed-paper discs, and seal with vinegar-proof lids. This keeps for a year. Refrigerate once opened.

My children tease me about the fastidiousness of my Christmas cookie decorating, but I take great pleasure in it. Pinterest is a great resource for inspiration.

Once I have a handle on gifts and shopping, I get into decorating, which is my favorite part of all. Whether we are home or away for Christmas, I always dress up our cottage to the nines. I love the notion of finding a Christmas tree to chop down on our farm, but having seen the wonky ones that grow naturally on our land, they leave me wanting a more traditionally shaped tree. So I buy one from our local village farmer, the price of which seems completely reasonable to me by New York City standards but never fails to shock my husband. I surrender an entire weekend to hanging lights and baubles on the tree and arranging garlands on the fireplace mantels and staircase railings. Beyond our house, I am usually in charge of decorations for my mother-in-law's sitting room and the big dining tables where we will all convene on Christmas Day, usually at my brother-in-law's house. As our cottage dining table only seats ten, I have never hosted the big Christmas meal, instead volunteering to pitch in wherever I am useful, mostly with making everything look pretty. Over the last four years, I have found my favorite places to buy ornaments and decorations and have figured out that you have to get there early to get the best selection. Now I have quite a healthy stock of twinkling lights, convincing-enough faux garlands, little wooden animal figures, and other tchotchkes that I then combine with real amaryllis from the nursery and real holly and old-man's-beard from around the farm to make a lovely and festive farm Christmas for all our family to enjoy.

We have spent four actual Christmas Days on the farm—one back in 2002 when Coco was a year and a half old and Zach was not yet born, and three since moving here. But even when we are off traveling over Christmas, we always find a day to celebrate the holiday all together as a family. A typical Christmas dinner includes those Brookses who actually live on the farm (thirteen at last count) plus extended family who live nearby or come to stay, and of course any close friends who choose to opt in as well. By trial and error, we have refined the Christmas schedule over the years, and I think we all agree that we now have it pretty much down to an exact science.

*I love a diverse Christmas tree. This one has ornaments from eBay, Liberty, Astier de Villatte, and assorted
travels around the world. My favorite part of the tree year after year, however, is the hand-strung
popcorn garland that Coco has taken over from me as her yearly contribution.*

December 23rd—Carol singing and cocktails at Sarsden chapel. Our neighbors to the north of the farm live in a big stately home with its own chapel, and this is where we gather with all our friends from the surrounding farms to celebrate Christmas. Everyone gets dressed up and I always look forward to wearing my favorite "Christmas" jacket—a black velvet and gold brocade Oscar de la Renta from the 1980s that was passed down to me by my mother. In the past few years, the service has featured a gospel choir, which I think shook up the old establishment at first, but now everyone has embraced it for the rockin' good time that it is.

December 24th—The day is focused on final decorations for Christmas lunch: setting the table, hanging more lights, making the fireplace mantels look festive and cozy. I love this day—everyone is around and pitching in to decorate, prepare food, and get in the mood for Christmas. It has typically been one of my favorite times spent together as a family. Then in the evening, I cook a roast beef for just our immediate family at home. Sometimes my mother-in-law joins us, or any family I might have visiting from the States.

December 25th—Well, of course the first thing we do is open presents at home and have a lovely breakfast. Zach and Coco still share the same bed on Christmas Eve and run downstairs first thing to check out the loot that has accumulated under the tree and in their stockings. Christopher's mother makes the rounds, dividing her attention among three households of children and grandchildren, stopping by for a coffee and hand delivering her presents for us. Then, anyone who wants to joins in for a family ride, some on horses, some on bikes. It's great to get a bit of fresh air. Around one p.m., we meet at my mother-in-law's house, where the adults have champagne and smoked salmon on toast, and the young cousins all exchange presents. Afterward we all head next door to Christopher's brother's house for a traditional Christmas lunch of roast turkey all together. No matter which part of the meal we're enjoying, we always turn on the TV to watch the Queen give her Christmas address. I love this English tradition.

Place cards that I bought in England for our family meal, but that remind me of the Crane's cards we used when I was growing up in Westchester.

On Christmas Eve, I like to do a different wintry theme so we don't overdose on red and green. The tablecloth and decorations came from Anthropologie, the Imari plates were passed down from my grandmother, the fringe napkins and rush place mats are English, and the white spotted glasses were a souvenir from a family trip we took to Venice.

December 26th—After two days of intensive family gathering on the farm, it's lovely to get out for a day of hunting. Sometimes I join Coco and Christopher at the Boxing Day meet, and other times I'll just go on foot with Zach and then we sneak home to eat leftovers before anyone else gets their hands on them.

December 27th—Off on an adventure! We typically don't stick around for New Year's Eve in England, usually choosing to go somewhere warm in order to store up heat and sunshine for the dark and chilly months to come.

When Christmas is over, I always enjoy realizing that the shortest day of the year is behind us. There will still be at least two more long months of winter ahead of us, but I am comforted in the knowledge that the days are getting longer slowly but surely.

CHAPTER VIII—JANUARY

*Hibernation – Taking a break from booze and sugar – Occasional snow –
Late sunrise – Resetting work habits – Giving the garden a haircut –
My weekly routine – Winter blossoms – Beagling – Bird shooting – Farm fashion –
Missing New York – Cold-weather cooking*

I considered myself warned about January when we moved to the farm. Friends who know England well had gone so far as to *sit me down* to talk about getting through even just one English winter, let alone the possibility and eventual reality of many of them. It would be dark when I woke up and for quite a while after, and it would be dark again way before bedtime, before dinner, even before I picked up my kids from school. One friend, a New York doctor who did his residency in Oxford, even told me that I should really consider getting an artificial light box, for both my health and my sanity in such a brooding, dark month.

Getting through my first January on the farm was kind of like going to a movie that had been given horrible reviews. My expectations were so low that I almost couldn't help but like it. First of all, in January we are already past the winter solstice, and the days are already starting to get longer again. And yes, the joy and celebration of Christmas is over and we are faced with two long months of bleak winter, but there is also a cozy feeling to having all the parties and the pressure of the holidays behind us and just embracing our hibernation.

THE FACE OF JANUARY EACH WAY LOOKS—
FLAMES THE FIRST CROCUS, ICE-TOPPED FLOW THE BROOKS.

And hibernate we do. I am a committed nondieter, but January is the one month where I apply a small amount of discipline to what I put in my body. My rules are simple: no processed sugar, no alcohol, but everything else, in every food group, is fair game—cheeseburgers, shepherd's pie, pasta—all good. I had been on this January program for five years by the time I arrived in England. In my life I have observed that sugar and alcohol are simply habits for me, ones that, without any boundaries, seem to increase over the course of the year.

So in January I like to hit the reset button and remind myself that I can, in fact, socialize without cocktails or get through an evening after a stressful day without a glass of wine. I have especially felt the need for a dry January since we moved to England. I still can't get over how much people drink here! Highly esteemed professionals find it totally acceptable to drink at a party until they have to be carried out. Slurring is par for the course, and blackouts are common. I'm not kidding! I still can't compete with any English person when it comes to drinking, but living here definitely increased my own habit. Wine at lunch, champagne before dinner, late-night drinks in the drawing room by the fire. So come January I am begging for mercy.

Sugar, on the other hand, is something I really don't crave unless I have been overindulging. I find that if I satisfy myself in my main meal, then I don't need anything to finish it off afterward. I admit that I am not so strict about the sugar—I still put honey in my tea, eat sweetened yogurt, and don't worry about my fruit intake—it's more about abstaining from the habit of dessert. But booze is off the menu entirely, and the result is that I sleep an impressive ten hours every night!

My healthy January was a lot easier to pull off in New York—the days were so busy and frantic that I could easily skip a meal or give myself dietary restrictions without involving a whole lot of torture. Christopher and I used to do a five-day juice fast when we felt like we needed to rein it in a bit. On the farm, however, life is more pleasurable and slow and focused on simpler indulgences—like food! and wine!—to give our lives quality. So any kind of restriction is not easy. That first January, after eating way more than I was ever used to in New York—and gaining ten pounds that I was okay with (and in fact probably looked better for) the idea of restricting myself was tougher than normal. But I did it. I like to think that I've gotten better each year that I've been here. I am working more and finding it easier to say no to social events if I feel I need a break, and the excitement of allowing myself wine at every meal if I felt like it (Okay, not at breakfast. And only at social lunches. But still.) has died down. A bit.

The cottage, all tucked into the unusually snowy landscape.

So, dinner at six p.m. Read a book in the bath at seven. Watch a TV show (binge-watching a series is *essential* in January) at eight, and lights out at nine-thirty. Quiet though it is, it's happy too. This moment—early to bed, early to rise—is when I most feel we live a "farmer's life," and to our surprise, we are all exhausted—as if awoken in the stark middle of the night—when the alarm goes off in the pitch black at 6:40 a.m.

In fact, if I find one thing unbearable about January it is waking in the dark. I hate it! It's very sad to be making coffee in the kitchen staring out the windows into blackness when it was already dark for five hours before we went to sleep the night before.

The first January we were here, there was snow on the ground for much of the winter, and it was very, very cold. Too cold. But more recent and typical Januarys have been relatively dry, and milder than I am used to in the States. Although I enjoy the snow, I have to say that I completely love a less painful (i.e., warmer) winter.

The early-morning view of January from my bedroom window.

What I am most grateful for in January are the incredible sunrises I get to see as I am starting my day. You don't see the sun emerge from the horizon until after eight a.m., and mornings are from time to time clear enough to watch the sky go from dark to pale pink, to orange, to streaked pink and blue, to yellow, and back to blue, all while having our breakfast and getting into our morning routine. One Sunday, the sky was so spectacular that I piled a heavy, warm coat over my pajamas, armed myself with a hot coffee in one hand and a camera in the other, and walked up to the pillars at the top of the farm to take some pictures. Even on days with rainy afternoons, Mother Nature often blesses us with beautiful January mornings. I can't tell you how happy it has made me to start the day off this way.

And speaking of starting the day, January is also about starting the year with good habits in my professional life as well as in my personal life. With the clarity that good sleep and a clear head affords me, I am focused on sticking to a work schedule that sets the tone for the months ahead. My main goal is to be as close to a fireplace as I can at all times. We have two in our house and one in my office, and for me, a roaring fire replaces the warmth and light from the sun in the winter months.

Because of the time spent indoors in the January weeks, we do our best to get outside on the weekends. There are always a few warm-enough weekend days in January to work in the garden. Because many plants stay green through December, in January it is time to give the garden a haircut. This might be my favorite work of the year in the garden. I love cutting, pruning, clipping, raking. Basically I thrive in any situation that involves tidying of any kind, and the garden is no exception. I am good at it, and it's immensely satisfying. Coco is not such a keen

The kids' living room in our cottage gets really warm when the fireplace is going, so I often camp out in here to write or answer e-mails on my laptop during the colder months.

green thumb, but I can usually convince Zach to join me. He loves pruning, and I'll get Christopher to clip the big things like the roses, buddleia, and philadelphus, and then I go around after them cleaning everything up. I make sure the tops of the freshly cut plants are even, pick up whatever debris they've left in the beds, rake old leaves, collect any large rocks that are sticking out, and just make everything look as orderly as possible.

What is lovely about getting rid of the dead stuff is that it leaves room to see what is coming alive in January. Yes! In England, things come alive in January, and it feels like such a miracle to me. In America, we have at least four or five months where we are surrounded by nothingness in the garden, but here there is never a completely dead month in the growing season. Usually the hellebore make an appearance toward the end of the month. We have an abundance of them, some new, some as old as the garden. Their subtlety—in pale shades of yellow, white, purple, pink, and green—works perfectly with the dim light and other quite dull colors around them. If they were too bright, they would look jarring next to their gloomy surroundings, but they are perfect.

My Weekly Work Schedule

Monday: "Be Your Own Intern Day," aka, Do admin in my office. Get through my physical (mail, bills, invitations, to-do list) and my digital (e-mail) in-boxes.

Tuesday/Thursday: Writing days. I often park myself somewhere near a fireplace on these days, warm and cozy with a cup of tea nearby at all times. In order to write, I have to feel far away from my desk and physically coddled. I could be at home in our living room on these days, or at Soho Farmhouse if I crave a change of scenery. (For more on my writing habits, see page 137 in the September chapter).

Wednesdays: Photo research/writing. I take more photographs than the average person, using them for articles and books I am writing and also for Instagram, so I carve time out of my week to make sure they are filed and organized so I can find them when I need them. I also switch gears in my writing and focus on the roles I play as a contributing editor at *Condé Nast Traveler* and *Architectural Digest*—pitching stories, following through on ideas, or writing articles.

Friday: Professional mom/wife day. I focus on home and family obligations on Fridays. This includes everything from organizing holidays and choosing materials for a new renovation project, to attending school meetings and buying groceries for the weekend.

Our herb garden on the side of the cottage. Can you see all the long grass growing in between the boxwood? It's a menace!
If the ground isn't too hard, winter is a good time to dig out the roots and get rid of most of the weeds.

The winter honeysuckle bush at the corner of our garden is always the first thing to bloom.

There is also a lovely bush on the edge of the garden that makes an early spring showing sometime in January. Some years she puts her pretty blossoms out too early in the year and they get burned by a cold snap, withering up until more reliably warm temperatures arrive. Other years, her little flowers flourish and she is one of the first to show her green leaves in the spring. Technically her name is *Lonicera fragrantissima,* but I prefer her many nicknames: winter honeysuckle, January jasmine, kiss-me-at-the-gate, and sweet-breath-of-spring.

Even though we are meant to be hibernating in January, some socializing is inevitable and it usually comes about in a sports-related way. Caroline hosts the beagling meet at our farm in January. Mostly oldies who

Hunting dogs love their job so much that when they get left behind it's heartbreaking for them. This beagle was found to have an injury once he arrived at the meet, so he had to stay put in the car for the day. He howled the whole time, poor guy.

have had to give up hunting for age-related reasons come, and they follow the beagles on foot. I am always proud to represent the Brooks family and help Caroline serve her guests in the backyard of her cottage. I pass around glasses of port and hot sausage rolls and say hello to all the friendly and exceedingly polite locals who are often curious to "meet Christopher's young, American wife." Ha!

Christopher and me on a pheasant shoot in Dorset. It was a particularly cold
and wet day and seemed to take days for me to warm up afterward.

Christopher waiting for grouse on the moor in Yorkshire. He was lucky to have a loader that day so he could use two guns and shoot consistently. Eating grouse on a shoot always makes me feel better about killing the birds.

We usually go away for a shooting weekend as well, and these occasions often put my sober social skills to the test. Shooting weekends are social marathons, and I occasionally find myself illicitly stuffing a cake in my mouth (despite the no-sugar rule) as a consolation for getting through five or six meals without any alcohol. But aside from those challenges, it's fun to spend time with friends, get outside in the fresh air, and have the excuse to get dressed to the nines for Saturday supper.

*Our cottage boot room, usually overwhelmed by Christopher's hoarding of outerwear for every occasion and chore
(but in this instance tidied up for a photo shoot). I got the framed soldiers from the Paris Flea Market.
I like how the repetition of the images creates order in the usual chaos of the room.*

In England I do sometimes miss getting dressed up. Like, *really* dressed up. But I have more chances to do so than you might think. I know farm life and black-tie parties don't really go hand in hand in the minds of most Americans, but thankfully in England they do! Once a month a friend (most likely one who lives in London and spends the weekends near us in the country) will host a formal dinner, which gives me the chance to wear a cocktail dress or a skirt and high heels. Similarly, big racing days like the Cheltenham Gold Cup or a day at Royal Ascot require a dressed-up look with a hat, which always produces a particular and pleasurable challenge for a formerly self-pronounced non–hat wearer like me. But what excites me most are the dinners at the more formal of the shooting weekends that we go to. Black tie in the countryside. I love the romance of it. I keep dreaming of the perfect velvet

Christopher and me on the hillside in Wales. This is how we typically dress in England on a daily basis. Nothing special, really.

gown that I will find and wear forever, just on those weekends. In the meantime, I have a little collection of long satin column skirts, feathered or sequin jackets, silk camisoles, and chandelier earrings that can be mixed and matched in any number of ways to make new looks.

The rest of the time I am in jeans, corduroy trousers, or jodhpurs (if I am riding) nearly every day, with or without a sweater and/or a wind/waterproof jacket, depending on the day. On my feet, I'm either wearing Le Chameau wellies (by far the most comfortable for walking) or, if the weather is more kind, tan suede Clarks Wallabees, which seem to be indestructible, and their flat crepe sole minimizes mud being tracked into the house.

The bottom line is that anything I wear on the farm, whether casual or dressy, in the day or evening, is likely to end up with mud on it. You should see me tiptoeing barefoot to the car on my way to a party carrying my nice shoes, desperately trying to keep them pristine. But the trouble is that both the outside and inside of my car, despite regular trips to the car wash, are always covered in mud and dust as well. It seems perfectly acceptable for men and women alike to walk into a country party with muddy shoes, which I find totally hilarious, but I just don't want to ruin mine, so I try my best to put them on at the last possible moment. Such are the trials of trying to be chic in the country.

My style in general has become much less trendy since moving here, and even though I am still not immune to a binge at Zara or an occasional designer purchase, the resulting look is pretty classic and traditional. What's funny to me is that my country friends who grew up around here are much more into wearing leather, studs, loud prints, and other pieces that convey a sense of "fashion." They often look at my tomboy English country look and say, "Sometimes it's hard to believe you worked in fashion for all those years."

My life in New York, specifically in the fashion industry, was, frankly, so full of adoration. Too much adoration. People wanted me to go to their parties, to their fashion shows. They wanted me to sit at their table. They wanted to dress me and send a car for me. They wanted to take my picture and quote my opinions. They wanted to send me free handbags and give me free meals, even free trips abroad! By the time I left, all of that had lost its value to me, or so I thought. It felt so easy to walk away from. Six years down the line, I'm crystal clear that I made the right decision, but I hadn't anticipated the shift in independence and development of individual self-esteem it would require. Mostly the fulfillment derived from walks alone with my dog, the creativity of cooking and making jam, and the attention I was able to give my husband and children seemed to be all I needed and wanted. But over time, I sometimes felt a sense of loneliness that was hard to accept or make sense of. I realized that from time to time I could feel the void that the lack of all that external attention left behind. Sometimes I would expect someone, anyone else, to fill it—Christopher, the kids, the farm, my friends—and I would be disappointed when they were not able to. It took me a while and a great deal of introspection to understand that the void needed to heal and not be refilled. Once I understood that, I became more patient with the discomfort I sometimes felt and learned to focus instead on the rightness of the choices I have made and all the many things I am so grateful for.

People ask me if I miss Fashion Week or if I miss the Met Ball. I honestly don't. I feel so full and so fulfilled from those occasions. I lived that life for a *long* time and at a formative age. I am so grateful that I waited until I absolutely could not go one more time to finally leave them behind, because I know for sure that I squeezed every single drop of fun and joy and excitement out of those events. I am simply left with a feeling of gratitude for having been included and for all the wonderful times I have had.

Zach and me in our downtime, walking on the gallops at sunset. Dressed for warmth and comfort.

With a quieter schedule in January, I also like to cook more. I'll make a double recipe of something like Roast Chicken with Vegetables (see page 216 for recipe) at the start of the weekend that can be eaten for Saturday lunch or dinner and again as leftovers on Sunday. I make a lot of soups—my favorite being adaptations of recipes from Franny's, my most-loved Italian restaurant in Brooklyn. They blessed us all with a cookbook called *Franny's: Simple Seasonal Italian* in 2013, and it has become my bible for soup, especially the Chickpea and Kale one. I often shy away from having soup as a whole meal—they typically just don't satisfy me enough—but this one does, and I have adapted Franny's instructions to make my own faster, easier version for days when I am in a hurry.

Chickpea and Kale Soup
From *Franny's: Simple Seasonal Italian*

Let me just admit that when I am in a rush, I substitute ready-made vegetable stock to eliminate the more time-consuming homemade version in this recipe and I also use canned chickpeas (essentially eliminating the first three paragraphs of this recipe). It cuts the cooking time way down, and the result is perfectly delicious, although when I do have the time, I enjoy following this recipe to the letter.

Makes 8–10 cups, 4–6 bowls

2 cups dried chickpeas
1 carrot, peeled and cut into large chunks
1 celery stalk
1 medium onion, halved
11 garlic cloves
5 strips lemon peel from an unwaxed lemon
1 rosemary sprig
1 tablespoon sea salt, or more to taste

3 1/2 quarts water
1 1/2 cups plus 2 tablespoons olive oil,
    plus more for drizzling
1/4 teaspoon chili flakes
2 bunches Tuscan kale
freshly cracked black pepper
lemon wedges
Parmesan cheese, finely grated

Place the chickpeas in a large bowl and cover with plenty of water. Let soak for 8 hours or overnight; drain.

    Wrap the carrot, celery, onion, 3 garlic cloves, lemon peel, and rosemary in a large square of cheesecloth and secure with kitchen twine or a large knot.

    In a large pot, combine the chickpeas, the sachet of vegetables, salt, water, and 1 cup of the olive oil. Bring to a boil over high heat, then reduce heat to medium-low and simmer until chickpeas are tender, about 1 hour.

    Meanwhile, finely chop the remaining garlic cloves. In a small skillet, heat 3 tablespoons of oil over medium heat. Add garlic and chili flakes and cook until garlic is fragrant but not golden, about 1 minute. Remove from heat.

    Remove the center ribs from the kale and coarsely chop the leaves (you should have about 16 cups). In a large skillet, heat the remaining 7 tablespoons of olive oil over medium-high heat. Add the kale in batches and cook, tossing occasionally, until tender, about 3 minutes. Remove from heat.

    When the chickpeas are cooked, combine the kale, garlic oil, 2 cups of chickpeas, and 1 cup of cooking liquid in a food processor and purée until smooth. Return the purée to the pot and cook over medium-high heat until hot. Season with salt and pepper to taste.

    Ladle the soup into cups or bowls. Finish with a squeeze of lemon, some grated Parmesan, and a drizzle of olive oil.

ROAST CHICKEN WITH VEGETABLES AND BREAD SAUCE
Adapted from Tamasin Day-Lewis's
Tamasin's Kitchen Bible

Tamasin's cookbook has been my go-to for classic, everyday English recipes since long before we moved here. She just makes everything in the most traditional, straightforward way, and does so exceptionally well. I have learned so many little tricks that I incorporate into my own cooking from her recipes. From this one I learned to always roast meat over a sliced onion or two. I now can barely eat any roasted meat if it is not accompanied by roast onions coated in drippings, and they are heaven to add to any kind of leftovers in the days that follow. This is my simplified version of Tamasin's Roast Chicken recipe.

SERVES 4–6

Roast Chicken and Vegetables:

3 1/4–4 1/2 pounds organic, free-range chicken
1 or 2 medium red onions
a few sprigs of rosemary, chopped
sea salt and black pepper
olive oil

1 organic lemon
carrots, potatoes, parsnips, and the like—
*   whatever root vegetables you have*
*   on hand—chopped*

Preheat the oven to 400°F. A chicken of this size will take an hour to an hour and a quarter to cook and then should rest to allow the juices to flood back through the meat.

Slice a large red onion (or two!) and lay the slices on the bottom of the roasting dish. Place the bird in the roasting dish and sprinkle with chopped rosemary. Season with salt and pepper and drizzle with olive oil. Lastly, squeeze lemon juice liberally all over the skin.

Place the pan on the bottom rack of the oven. After 15 minutes, add the root vegetables and use a baster to cover with cooking juices, basting every so often. Season with salt and pepper. After 45 minutes, if you insert a skewer into the deep part of the leg and the meat juices run clear rather than bloody, the bird is cooked. If not, leave for 15 minutes longer. Remove it from the roasting pan with a carving knife and fork. Leave it to rest on the carving board with foil tucked around it and a tea towel on top for 15 minutes before carving.

At this point most people would turn to making their gravy, but in our house we have all come to prefer Bread Sauce, an English classic.

Bread Sauce:

1 small onion, peeled and stuck with 4 cloves
1 bay leaf
2 cups whole milk
pinch of ground nutmeg

sea salt and black pepper
1 small loaf white or whole-wheat bread, crusts
removed, torn into smallish shreds
1 teaspoon salted butter (optional)

Place the cloved onion in a small saucepan with the bay leaf and milk and bring slowly to just below the boiling point. Lower the heat and simmer for 20–30 minutes, adding a pinch of nutmeg halfway through. Season, and add the torn bread by the handful until most, but not all, of the milk has been absorbed. Remove from heat and leave to one side, covered, for 20 minutes.

Just before serving the chicken, take off the lid and if the sauce looks too solid, add a little more milk. Test the seasoning and add more salt, pepper, or nutmeg as desired. Stir in the butter if you want a richer sauce. Remove the onion and bay leaf, and serve the sauce in a small pitcher.

We always make room for a Sunday Roast Pork (I capitalize it because it is *that* important) in January. When I first started spending summers in England, at the tender age of twenty-three, roast pork was among the very first things I learned to make. I decided to teach myself cooking because I was bored. Christopher was out on his tractor being a farmer all day, which surprised me because in New York I thought of him as an edgy, Lower East Side artist and now he was suddenly wearing a Carhartt onesie and tweed cap, tending to his land. I have to admit, I liked the dichotomy, although it did leave me feeling lonely more than once. He had no shame about setting off after breakfast and not appearing again until suppertime. And this was our vacation together! At first, I thought, "How lovely. I have some time to myself. I'll take a long bath and then give myself a manicure." But that was over in two hours—and then what? So I decided I would teach myself to cook. Christopher was very excited by this idea and suggested I start with his favorite English meal: roast pork with crackling. I didn't even know what crackling was but soon learned that it's the inch-thick piece of skin that the butchers don't remove here in England. When roasted, crackling becomes crusty and crunchy, and I dare say it tastes even better than bacon. At that point, since I was too scared to drive on the left side of the road, Christopher drove me to Slatters, our local butcher where the owner, Martin, who grew up with Christopher, sold us the perfect locally reared piece of pork loin. Home we went with our purchases, which also included some cabbage to sauté and potatoes to roast, and we stopped at Christopher's mother's house along the way to collect a recipe. Caroline gifted me her extra copy of *Delia's Complete Cookery Course*— the quintessential guide to English cooking by Delia Smith—and then I was all set to make my first truly English meal. Reflecting back now, what I remember most from that meal was my first taste of crackling. Our mutual joy at the flavor of crispy, melted pork fat was similar to hearing that we were pregnant with our first child—a shared euphoric satisfaction.

In all the summers and holidays we would eventually spend in England before moving here full time, we never missed a chance to have this favorite meal, and we still don't, especially in January, when we are in our collective family cave and have the time and energy to put into a big weekend meal. Christopher's friend Julian has become a part of the tradition along the way, often coming down after work on a Saturday afternoon, spending the night, and then partnering with me in the kitchen before a long, indulgent Sunday lunch. The kids have joined in with their enthusiasm, too, although Coco's love of pork was cut short by her decision, at the precocious age of seven, to stop eating meat entirely, deferring to her love of animals. Now age sixteen, when people ask her what she misses most about eating meat, invariably she answers: "Roast pork is the *only* thing I miss."

Sunday Roast Pork Lunch with Potatoes, Cabbage, and Gravy

Adapted from Tamasin Day-Lewis's
Tamasin's Kitchen Bible

I love a pork chop. I really do. In fact, I would say it's one of my favorite things to both cook and eat. However, English roast pork and crackling is just on a whole other level. Roasting a whole piece of meat holds in the juices more effectively and, combined with the rich, crispy, flavorful crackling, is a dish that, for me, is irresistible.

A note on buying the pork: make sure the meat has all its skin left on and that the fat has been properly scored. You can ask the butcher to do this for you.

Serves 6–8

Roast Pork:

4 1/2– 5 1/2 pounds leg or shoulder of organic or free-range pork
sea salt and black pepper

olive oil
1 medium onion, sliced

If you remember, season the meat with salt and pepper the night before you're going to cook it. When you've brought it up to room temperature on the day of preparation, rub the crackling with a little olive oil with your fingers and sprinkle salt all over it.

Preheat the oven to 425°F. Place the joint on the onion in a roasting pan and cook for 30 minutes. Then turn the heat down to 325°F. Calculate the overall cooking time of the joint at 35 minutes per pound.

If the crackling hasn't achieved the heights of crackle that you would wish for at the end of the cooking time, remove it with a long, thin-bladed knife all in one piece and place it under a hot grill. Keep a close eye on it so it doesn't burn. Alternatively, turn the oven temperature back up to its original heat and place the roasting pan with the joint in it at the top of the oven for a further 10–15 minutes. Remove the joint in the normal way and allow it to rest for 15 minutes while you make the gravy and finish off the vegetables. This is not, however, a joint to cover. The crackling will get soggy from condensation if you do, so just keep the meat warm somewhere. Make sure to save all of the cooking juices and onion for the gravy. In addition to the gravy, serve the pork with your favorite applesauce.

Roasted Potatoes:

Yukon gold potatoes (1 potato per person)   *goose or duck fat, or 3–4 tablespoons olive oil*

Peel the potatoes and cut into quarters. Place in a large pan, cover with cold, salted water, cover, and bring to a boil. Remove the lid and boil rapidly for about 5 minutes, by which time the potatoes will not be totally resistant when you poke a knife tip into them. Place a colander over a large jug or bowl. Drain the potatoes into the colander, reserving the water for the gravy (allow the water to sit still to let the starches drift to the bottom of the container). I give the colander a little shake to fluff up the floury surface of the potatoes so that more fat adheres to them.

A couple of minutes before you drain the potatoes, place a large roasting pan with a generous hunk (a well-heaped tablespoon plus a bit more) of goose or duck fat or 3–4 tablespoons of olive oil in the top rack of the oven and wait until you hear it splutter, 3–4 minutes. Olive oil makes good, crisp roast potatoes, but the flavor imparted from fat dripping is infinitely superior.

Transfer the roasting pan to the stovetop and slip the drained potatoes into it, standing back, as they will begin to splutter madly. Turn each potato chunk in the fat so that they are completely coated.

Return the pan to the oven and roast for about 1 hour, turning every 20 minutes as each side crisps. When they are crisp all over and the rest of the lunch is ready to put on the table, drain the fat and plop the potatoes into a heated serving dish.

Gravy:

juices and caramelized onion from the
    roast pork

red wine
water reserved from the boiled potatoes

You already have the caramelized onion from under the pork and the meat juices in the pan. Place the pan over high heat, add a good splash of red wine to deglaze, about a half cup if you have some open, and stir like crazy so that the sticky onions part company with the pan and break down even further, releasing their flavor and dark color. Let the wine bubble away merrily for a minute or two to let the alcohol burn off, then add the cooking water from the potatoes. You won't want to use all the potato water, so pour most of it down the drain until you have about a cup left with all the starchy part, which will thicken the gravy. Pour it into the pan and boil over high heat for 5 minutes more to reduce the sauce. Place a sieve over a large jug and set it in the sink. Pour in the gravy and force through as much of the delicious debris as you can with a wooden spoon, and then pour into a fat/lean gravy pitcher (where one side releases the fat with the gravy and the other side pours fat-free)!

Sautéed Savoy Cabbage:

This is my own recipe. I always cook the whole head of cabbage and usually eat the leftovers cold out of the fridge when I need a snack.

1 head savoy cabbage (or virtually any green
    variety)
2 tablespoons extra-virgin olive oil

1 tablespoon salted butter
sea salt and black pepper

Turn the cabbage on its side and cut the whole head into slices from top to bottom. When you get to the core, work your way around it, leaving out the hard middle part. Heat the oil and butter in a pan over medium-high heat until it is sputtering, then add the cabbage and season with salt and pepper. I like to leave the heat on medium-high for a few minutes to really brown the parts of the cabbage that are sitting on the bottom of the pan, and then I turn it down to medium-low to let it all cook through, stirring occasionally, until soft. Serve piping hot.

The last week in January is probably my sanest week of the year. I've had plenty of sleep and downtime, I've read lots, watched a satisfying amount of TV, had enough hot baths and roaring fires to keep me warm; my sober mind is focused, my blood sugar is stable, I've seen enough friends to not feel isolated, and I've gotten a lot of work done—both in and around the house, in my office, and in the garden. I often ask myself, at the end of January, "Why live any other way?" But soon enough, the predictability of routine and discipline gets a bit boring, the social swing picks up again, and the desire to live a bit of a less-controlled life overwhelms me. Then the other eleven months of the year unfold as they will.

Late-January sunrise in the field that separates Fairgreen and Castle Barn Farms.

CHAPTER IX—FEBRUARY

Early spring bulbs – The joys of the John Deere Gator – Sunrise walks –
Snow – What winter is like – Meals from home – Farm repairs

FEBRUARY is the true marathon stretch of winter in England. The coziness of winter has become less compelling, and the subtle signs of spring are purely dependent on the weather. In warmer years, you see daffodils making an early appearance, but in colder ones you have to wait until March. The one guarantee in February are the snowdrops. Right at the beginning of the month, if not a week or two before, snowdrops start pushing their white blooms up through the soil. As we don't get snow here regularly, a couple of years ago Christopher undertook the arduous but ultimately gratifying task of planting sixteen thousand snowdrop bulbs—yes, *sixteen thousand*—in order to blanket our farmyard in the illusion of snow. I imagine we will be thanking him for our February beauty for generations to come.

WITH FEBRUARY THAWS AND RAINBOWS COME;
WHITE SNOWDROPS GLEAM, THE BIRDS NO MORE ARE DUMB.

Zach jumping ship from the Gator, probably because Coco was being bossy and not letting him drive.

It's hard to get the kids motivated to get outside on the cold winter weekends unless there is snow, which is a novelty. So I typically resort to the usual screen-related bribes. *If you bike with me for forty-five minutes, we can come home and watch a movie.* When we first moved to the farm, I noticed with great relief how much less time we all spent looking at a screen. In fact, a month after we arrived, we got a phone message from Virgin Airlines letting us know that Coco had left her laptop on the plane after our journey from America . . . she hadn't even noticed! This intense focus on our new surroundings lasted for a while, maybe a little more than a year, I'd say, and then as the kids got older and got phones, and as Christopher and I dedicated more time to working than being on sabbatical, and as we all got addicted to Instagram, we all got stuck back in our old ways. I wish this wasn't the case, but it is. I get romantic ideas from time to time that I'll leave my phone in the house during the day to try to manage the compulsive habit of looking at it all the time, but it just doesn't happen consistently.

The more appealing outdoor activity, which requires less manipulation, is a driving lesson on the John Deere Gator. Who doesn't *love* a four-wheel, open-air farm vehicle? My husband certainly does—especially because it's electric, so it doesn't make that loud humming diesel noise that disrupts the peace. In fact, it was the first thing we bought when we moved here. He even did his research at our local John Deere shop on Long Island before the decision to move was final. Come to think of it, Christopher's excitement about getting a Gator could have been a large factor in his support of our moving here!

Our new Gator arrived at the farm long before we had finished unpacking, set up reliable Wi-Fi, or gotten the kids settled into school. Even though I dismissed it as nothing more than a guy toy, I have to now humbly admit that it's probably the most useful piece of equipment we have on the farm. Our groom, Sinead, uses it to deliver hay to the horses; our builder, Tomak, carts endless heavy building materials around the farmyard with it; and Christopher often loads it up with heavy furniture or equipment to move between buildings. It wasn't long before the kids thought they ought to give it a try. After Coco proved to me that she was capable of looking both ways where the driveways intersected and maintaining a sensible speed, she was allowed the privilege, at age twelve, of driving it up to her grandma's for a meal or to her aunt and uncle's house for a tennis lesson. Both are just a quarter mile up the farm driveway, but still, at first I had butterflies. Now we often spend winter weekends giving the kids driving lessons on the Gator. It gives them a good bit of fresh air and adrenaline, and the discipline derived from refining a skill. Also, Ginger goes completely over the top with excitement at the

chance to chase the Gator. It must emit some sound that only dogs can hear, because the minute you turn it on she starts barking as if her life depended on it. It's
become a good way to give her some exercise and eventually tire her out as well.

I haven't let Zach near a car yet, but around age thirteen or fourteen Coco asked
if she could try driving the old beat-up Subaru Forester (for some reason a must-
have car for all farm owners in the Cotswolds) around the farm, and when I con-
sented, she got in the car with me and off she went. Driving! Just like that!

Sometimes the weather is so bleak in February that a whole week can go by without spending any time outdoors other than going to and from the car. After a
while, I can just feel myself shrinking into my surroundings and the hibernation
of winter starts to feel more like claustrophobia. I often don't realize how much
I am craving the sun until it makes an appearance, and like a zombie I find myself
walking outside as if by calling, as opposed to free will.

Since Zach has started at boarding school, my newfound freedom in the mornings has been almost startling. No 6:40 a.m. alarm bell, no rushed breakfast, no
forty-minute school run. So I started making a conscious effort to savor my new
start-of-the-day options. Sometimes I lie in bed reading a book or chatting with
Christopher like we used to do on the weekends before we had kids; sometimes
I go to my office early to get a head start on a new creative project that requires
energy I only seem to have at the start of the day. I often take the time to make
myself a leisurely breakfast. But when we are in mid-February and the sun comes
up into the sky a little earlier, the timing is right for a longer walk up the hill from
our cottage to watch the sun rise before I get started on my daily routine. Usually
Ginger and I set off up the bridle path, and Fatboy might follow us for a while.
He's the more intrepid of the two cats, often following us at least as far as the
edge of the farm borders.

It's strange how all three of our domestic animals tend to know exactly where our
farm ends and only Gingy will cross over, though she has to be with someone of
authority (meaning not the children). So as we pass over the gallops and through
the old pillars, the sun is usually just coming up over the horizon. Ginger and I
stand together, both absorbing the light and the warmth, until it is too bright to
face directly. Then we walk back down toward home, where I make soft-boiled
eggs, toast, and, on occasion, fresh-squeezed blood orange juice, and then I am
ready to get to work. And to face the rest of February.

Gingy catching her breath in a frosty field after running up the hill from the cottage.

Remnants of Zach's enthusiasm for snow.

On the rare occasion that snow does fall on the farm, it often comes in February. During our first year living in England, both Zach and Coco had a whopping three days off from school because of the snow. This did not seem so out of the ordinary to me, having spent all of my school years in New York, western Massachusetts, and Rhode Island—all typically snow-heavy states. But I have since realized that it was. So rare, in fact, that it hasn't happened again. Not even once. I can count on one hand the times that it has snowed in the past five years, and it's been a pretty modest dump every time: a little dusting here, an inch or two there. Certainly nothing to stay home from school for.

The winter of 2014–15 was particularly cruel. New York was getting a weekly dump of major snow and endless snow days—which gave Zach, my little snow-lover, one more reason to be homesick—and in England we just got the odd flurry here and there. So after three snowless winters, we resolved in 2016 to take the kids skiing on their February school break. I never thought I'd say that I craved winter once I moved to England, but when we arrived in the French Alps for a week of snow and skiing, I knew that I had.

I'm slowly realizing that England is more seasonless than I had imagined. It could be 50 degrees in midsummer as easily as it could be the same 50 degrees in midwinter. In New York, you can pretty much bank on the temperature being warm enough to swim in June, July, and August, and you can rely on it being mostly below freezing in January and February. I know the weather has been more of an anomaly than we are all used to in the past five years, but still—in the American Northeast, you can pretty much expect that there are going to be four seasons with the random wild card days from time to time. Here in England, that is most certainly not the case. July and August could go by entirely with nothing better than drizzle, clouds, and sweater-wearing temperatures. And the winter, as I've just described, might hardly go below freezing. I knew I'd have to get away for some *real* sun and warmth, but as a girl who never, ever complains about the heat, I didn't figure I'd be eventually craving colder weather as well.

No matter the extremes, or lack thereof, of the outside temperatures, February is always still winter in my kitchen. With our social lives getting back in swing, I'll often invite our commuter friends—those who live in London during the week and come to their country houses in our 'hood on the weekends—over for a rich wintry meal on a Saturday night. Chicken Potpie is my go-to for these evenings. Any kind of meat pie is inherently English, but I like to serve my strictly American version. The idea came to me after a visit to the Le Creuset store at Bicester

Village, the nearby outlet mall and the closest thing I have to New York City shopping at the farm. On final sale were these little mini-cocottes, as they call them, little tiny versions of the signature Le Creuset Dutch oven. They are so damn cute I had to have them. I hemmed and hawed about what color to get—I eventually chose classic white—and also settled on the slightly larger oval version, figuring they were better for main course serving. When I got home, I excitedly flipped through the recipe book that came with them and got a rush when I saw the potpie recipe. But the Le Creuset recipe had pearl onions in it and that freaked me out. I have a very set idea of what ingredients should go in my Chicken Potpie, and I decided their recipe was trying too hard to be fancy. Then a brilliant idea came to me as I wondered whom I could rely on for a straightforward, reliable, no-nonsense but guaranteed good classic American recipe. Of course! *The Silver Palate Cookbook*! I googled it, scanned the required ingredients for anything that seemed out of place, and printed it out when I was assured it was as old-school as I had in my mind. I wasn't disappointed, and neither were my guests. It's now become a winter staple, a crowd-pleaser, and my own unique, American way of serving something typically English.

CHICKEN POTPIE
Adapted from Julee Rosso and Sheila Lukins's
The Silver Palate Cookbook

SERVES 6

Filling:

1 ¹/₂–2 pounds boneless,
*   skinless chicken breasts*
1 cup heavy cream
3 medium red potatoes, cut into 1-inch chunks
4 carrots, peeled and thinly sliced
5 tablespoons unsalted butter
1 large yellow onion, chopped
5 tablespoons flour

1 cup chicken broth
¹/₄ cup dry white wine
1 tablespoon dried tarragon
2 teaspoons fresh thyme
*   (or 1 teaspoon dried)*
1 teaspoon sea salt
¹/₂ teaspoon ground black pepper
³/₄ cup frozen green peas

Crust:

1 package frozen puff pastry, thawed

1 egg
1 teaspoon water

Preheat the oven to 350°F. Place the chicken in a baking dish in a single layer. Pour the cream over the chicken and bake for 25–40 minutes, depending on the size of the chicken breasts. Remove the chicken from the cream, reserving the cream for the sauce. Once the chicken has cooled, cut it into 1-inch pieces.

Place the potatoes in a pot of cold water and bring to a boil. After 10 minutes, add the carrots and cook 5–10 minutes more, until both the potatoes and the carrots are fork-tender. Drain and set the vegetables aside.

Melt the butter in a wide sauté pan over medium heat, add the onion, and cook until translucent. Sprinkle in the flour; stir and cook 5 minutes, but do not brown. Slowly add the broth to the onion mixture, whisking until the sauce smooths out and thickens. Add the reserved cream, white wine, tarragon, thyme, salt, and pepper and cook 5 minutes more. Add the chicken, potatoes, carrots, and frozen peas to this sauce and mix gently. Pour the mixture into 6 large ramekins (or mini-cocottes!) for individual potpies.

Preheat the oven to 425°F. Roll out the pastry sheet and cut to fit the ramekins or cocottes. Press down the pastry edges. Beat together the egg and water, and brush over the top of the pastry to give a nice glossy finish to the crust. Bake for 25 minutes until golden brown. I always serve this with an Arugula Salad on the side (see page 61 for recipe).

INDIAN-INSPIRED LENTIL SOUP

Another American recipe that fits right into my farm life is my childhood babysitter's Lentil Soup recipe. Genevieve Amarantides lived around the corner from us in Bronxville, and she worked in our house from when I was four until I was twenty. Primarily she was there to look after my sister and me, but as we grew older and more independent, she took on more of the cooking duties in the kitchen. Genevieve was Greek, so we called her Yeno, an abbreviation of her Greek name. Yeno was the master soup maker in our family, and when I got married, she handed down all her recipes to me, with the lentil one being my favorite. Over the years, I have made her recipe my own with the addition of coconut milk, ginger, and a bit of curry powder, but I still add her secret ingredient—a drizzle of balsamic glaze over the hot soup just before taking my first bite. Every time I make it, I feel like I am right back at home in my childhood kitchen with Yeno at my side.

SERVES 4–6

olive oil
1 medium yellow onion
2 carrots
2 stalks celery
2 garlic cloves
sea salt
1/2 fennel bulb, chopped
1/2 teaspoon dried curry

1/2 teaspoon ground cumin
1/2 teaspoon ground turmeric
1 teaspoon freshly grated ginger
1 1/2 cup green lentils
2 generous handfuls of baby kale
1 scant cup coconut milk
juice of 1 lemon
balsamic glaze, for drizzling

Set a heavy-bottomed soup pot on the stove and add a couple of glugs of olive oil. Begin warming the oil over low heat as you chop vegetables. Chop the onion, carrots, and celery, making relatively uniform pieces. Smash the garlic, then roughly chop those as well. Turn the stove up to medium heat, then add the chopped vegetables, garlic, and a generous pinch of salt to the pot. Stir frequently as the vegetables soften and become fragrant. Add the fennel and cook for a few minutes more.

Add the spices and ginger to the mixture and stir for a minute, until spices are toasted and aromatic.

Add the lentils to the pot and 4–5 cups of water, depending on how thick you prefer your soup. Raise the temperature to high and allow the soup to come to a boil. Reduce heat to low and simmer uncovered for 25–30 minutes, until lentils are just tender but not mushy.

When lentils are almost tender, add the baby kale—they'll only take a minute or two to wilt. As soon as the greens are wilted and bright green, stir in the coconut milk, and then remove the pot from the heat. Finish with a lot of freshly squeezed lemon juice, a pinch of salt, and a drizzle of fruity olive oil. My own quirk is adding a drizzle of balsamic glaze, but a dollop of cold plain Greek yogurt works well too.

Raspberry Shrub

I don't yet have anything on the farm to harvest, so I turn to the barn freezer to see what I have saved for winter. I almost always have an abundance of frozen raspberries or blackberries from the summer, and I use them to make shrub, a drinking vinegar that when poured over a glass of icy Pellegrino makes a refreshing drink and reminds me of sunnier days. Making shrub couldn't be simpler.

1 cup raspberries, fresh or frozen
1 cup granulated sugar
1 cup red wine vinegar

Combine the raspberries and sugar in a glass bowl or lidded container. Stir to combine.

Cover and refrigerate overnight. Use a fine mesh sieve to strain out all raspberry solids. Discard the solids.

Combine the raspberry mixture with the vinegar and heat in a saucepan over medium-high heat, stirring until the sugar dissolves. Transfer to a glass jar and keep refrigerated.

To use the shrub in a drink, fill a glass with ice, add 2 tablespoons (or more to taste) of shrub, and top with sparkling water and a squeeze of lemon juice. Enjoy!

Rice Pudding

2 ounces pudding rice
3 tablespoons sugar (I prefer demerara)
1 bay leaf

1 vanilla bean, split and scraped
4 1/4 cups milk
5 ounces clotted cream

Preheat the oven to 285°F.

Place the rice into a baking dish with the sugar, bay leaf, vanilla pod and seeds, and half of the milk. Bake in the oven for one hour, then remove from the oven and stir in the remaining milk and discard the vanilla pod.

Return to the oven and bake for one hour more, or until the rice is soft and all the liquid has been absorbed.

Stir in the clotted cream and serve immediately.

*Dry stone walling is an ancient and revered craft in England. I love getting to see
how it's done close up when they get repaired on the farm.*

February is also a month of repairs. The cold, wet weather makes it necessary to repair the roads and driveways on the farm. We often just put down gravel in potholes until we have to take more serious measures, like repaving patches or, on occasion, a whole stretch. In 2015, we repaved a whole half-mile section of the driveway at the top of the farm—a major dent in the annual budget! Winter also can wreak havoc on the dry stone walls around our fields, and we often repair those in February, as long as we get a decent dry spell.

Dry stone walling is an impressive and incredible craft in and of itself. The entire wall is constructed using only limestone, without grout or any bonding substance at all to hold the individual stones in place. They are carefully hand-selected so that they fit together well enough to create strength to build upon and hold the entire wall in one piece. Because limestone is porous, it draws in moisture, which, when frozen, causes the stone to expand and contract, eventually cracking the stones, or *spalling*, as farmers call it. When the wall repairman is working on the farm, I often pull over to watch him do his impressive and fascinating work. It is a beautiful practice, and one that reminds me of why I love living on a farm. February is often a good time for such a reminder.

While the main farm drive is asphalt for practical reasons, our own driveways are made from limestone for aesthetic reasons, and they always require filling and repairs during and after the winter.

CHAPTER X—MARCH

*Birth of the lambs – Juice, our bottle lamb – Spring blooms –
Christopher's birthday – Weekend adventures – Lighter cooking –
Wild garlic – Plows in the fields*

MY favorite thing about March is the birth of the lambs. My brother-in-law has a small flock of black sheep, and every year about six of them are taken for a visit with the ram in November. Theoretically the lambs are meant to arrive about 147 days later, although this kind of precision never seems to be the case. Whenever we think the lambs will arrive, we end up waiting and waiting and waiting, until we sometimes give up on waiting. More than once I have been driving Zach to school or on my way to run an errand, and as I drive by the sheeps' field, I'm surprised to see a little lamb stumbling around trying to find his mother's teat.

WILD MARCH IS LOUD WITH WIND AND MATING SONG;
SWEET HER WHITE VIOLETS AS THE DAY IS LONG.

Christopher, age ten, holding Pimple, his bottle lamb.

For me, the thrill of holding newborn lambs has never worn off. When I was a teenager, my father's version of a midlife crisis compelled him to temporarily leave his hometown of Palm Beach, Florida, and buy a farm in Virginia, along with quite a large flock of sheep to tend on his own. It was often lambing season when I visited him there at spring break, and I loved to help mother the babies, especially when one or two needed extra milk, which we fed them from a bottle. My dad allowed us to name the girls, as they would stick around for breeding, but he always discouraged us from growing close to the males, as they were the ones that were quickly sent off to market. Once, though, a male lamb's mother abandoned him and we had to raise him in the house. We bathed him, cradled him, and fed him. My father was adamant we didn't name him, but we had to call him something, so he became "Number 19," after the tagging label on his ear, and when Number 19 eventually went to market, I rebelled by not eating lamb for two years.

When Christopher and I moved to England, I felt a similar excitement when lambing season arrived. For hours on end, I'd go sit in the lambing shed, where mothers and babies spend the first few days away from hungry, predatory foxes until the lambs are strong enough to be out in the open field. I still visit often. The ewe glares at me while I hold the lambs, trying so hard to include myself in this new little family, and nothing makes me happier than when Rob, who is in charge of lambing on the farm, lets me know that a newborn needs some supplemental milk. I pretend that it's going to be such a pleasure for the kids to bottle-feed them when they get home from school, but secretly I'm pretty sure it's me who enjoys it the most.

This birthing process happens over and over throughout March and into April. Every week or so, a new family enters the shed, hangs out for a few days, and then eventually starts its life in the field. Once in the field, we don't really have anything to do with lambs anymore. Even the days-old youngsters run away when you approach and are nearly impossible to catch—just trying upsets them too much. And the lambs grow up practically overnight. Before I know it, the young ones are impossible to distinguish from their mothers. I am grateful for the detachment; otherwise I don't think I'd be able to eat them. And I do eat them. I take pride in eating meat from animals who have been so loved and well raised. I actually can't think of any situation in which I would feel better about eating meat. That doesn't mean that my heart doesn't sink when I am cradling a baby male in my arms, knowing that he might end up in my stomach, but it does mean I can love him while I have the chance to.

One spring, I gave bottle supplements to a particularly frail lamb. She was a twin, but seemed to be much weaker than her sibling, having trouble even standing up long after she should have been walking. I thought this might be a case where someone would have to bring her inside to raise her on the bottle, as she and her mother were not bonding and she was barely strong enough to lift herself off the ground. Rob felt we should give her another day or two, and so we did. But on the second day, he found her lifeless in the shed. I was so sad that we hadn't tried harder to save her and that we had missed the chance to raise a lamb ourselves. Even though she likely wouldn't have made it in any case, I was filled with regret for weeks afterward.

Zach at the same age, having his own moment with a baby lamb, although this one got to stay with his mother.

The next spring, I made it clear to Rob that we were ready and willing to take in a lamb at the first sign of distress—not that I wanted it to be taken away from its mother unnecessarily, but that if its health was in question we would be more than delighted to step in.

Not long after, over the Easter holidays, Coco was home from school and had chosen to spend the morning at her cousin's house. I checked in with her mid-morning, and she said they were in the shed with the new lambs who were born in the night. It had been a particularly rough night for lambing, as it was unseasonably cold and we'd had a rare April snow shower just before bedtime that didn't thaw until the morning. In the late afternoon, Coco hadn't returned home, so I went up to my brother-in-law's to look in on her. Coco was sitting on the kitchen floor with a tiny lamb who had become terribly weak due to the cold weather in the night and not receiving enough milk from his mother. She had looked after his twin but appeared overwhelmed at the idea of being in charge of two. He lacked the strength to stand up, so Coco was holding him, surrounded by blankets, a bottle, and a bag of powdered lamb formula. They had already been to the farmshop to buy all the supplies needed to raise a bottle lamb at home. After a few hours inside to warm up and drink some bottled colostrum (the mother's thick first milk loaded with essential vitamins and minerals), Coco had taken him back outside to try bonding again with his mother. No luck. The ewe wasn't having it.

So that evening we brought home our baby boy. Yes, he was a boy, so our first conversation with both Christopher and his brother was to decide that, regardless of what would come of our lamb, whether he would stay in our farmyard as a pet or eventually go back and join the pack, he was not going to be slaughtered for meat. Not very farmerlike of us, I know, but living on a farm with as many animals as we do, we get our fair share of heartbreak and sadness, so I just didn't see the point in creating any unnecessary pain for me or the kids. With those assurances in place, Coco named him Juice, and he moved into our house. The first few nights were like having a newborn baby—he slept in our bedroom and we got up every few hours to feed him his bottle. After three days, Coco went back to school and Christopher went on a ten-day business trip, so I pretty much became Juice's sole caretaker in those formative first weeks. He wore a diaper and followed me everywhere, never allowing more than six inches between us, except at night when he slept in a dog crate. The cats never took to Juice, but Ginger, at first skeptical, threatened, and dismissive, actually came to enjoy Juice's company, running around the garden with him and treating him like a puppy.

When Ginger met Juice. Poor Gingy gave me this pleading and desperate look the whole first week that Juice was in the house. It took her a few more weeks after that to even make eye contact with Juice. Eventually, though, they became friends.

Having a cuddle with my teenage baby.

Eventually Juice graduated to living in an enclosed courtyard outside our cottage, and then to a yard in the stables across from our house. We'd often let him run around freely during the day, until the garden started coming into bloom and he got into the habit of eating every single flower in sight. But still, when we took Ginger, and in the summer months the foxhound puppies, out for their evening walk, Juice would join us and follow Ginger absolutely everywhere along the footpath, up the gallops, down the road, and back through the fields to the cottage, sometimes covering more than a mile. As he was weaned from the bottle, Juice stopped more often to eat grass along the way, and when I called him, just like a dog, he would ignore me for a minute or two and then come bounding up behind me at top speed to catch up. I was impressed even then by how fast he could run, but his true inner Usain Bolt was revealed when he developed another habit taught to him by Ginger—running behind the car when we left the farmyard to go somewhere. The first time he did it, I thought I'd outpace him pretty quickly, like I do with Ginger, but I soon had to stop when I realized that he was running as fast as I could drive on the bumpy dirt road. I had to drive back to the stables and lock him up in his yard before setting off again. Over time it's become apparent that Juice is just obsessed with my car, period. Once, I looked out my bedroom window and noticed that he was licking his way around the exterior bottom half of my car. I could tell by the marks he left on the muddy outside that he had in fact licked his way around the whole damn thing. WTF? Another time, Juice was in a paddock with one of the pigs when he saw my car coming up the driveway and got so excited that he jumped and cleared a four-foot stone wall to come and meet me. Crazy animal. It's obvious he identifies more as a dog than a sheep. In fact, one day while walking Ginger and Juice (Gin 'n' Juice) we decided to put Juice in with the other ewes and now grown-up lambs to see if he might be happier with his own kind and more company. They all approached with enthusiasm as Juice and I stood there on the edge of the field. Juice got nervous and looked back at me and ran around behind me to protect himself. In fact, we tried this twice, and both times he didn't show one ounce of interest in his own kind. A third time, we made a more serious attempt to reintroduce Juice to his flock. Worried that Juice was lonely in a yard by himself, we caught another sheep in the field and brought him in to live with Juice, who remained completely uninterested over the course of many weeks. Nonetheless, we eventually put the two of them back in the field with the rest of the sheep. Minutes later, Juice was

Juice getting carried back to his yard after eating most of the tulip heads in our garden. Christopher was not happy with him.

back home in the farmyard. He had jumped the wall surrounding the field and come straight back home. After four more attempts during which Juice jumped the wall again, as well as a five-bar gate and a similarly high wooden fence, we surrendered to the realization that Juice's will to come home to us was stronger than our will for him to be an actual sheep.

Anyway, Juice is all grown up now and still lives in our farmyard with a rotation of chickens, bunnies, pigs, dogs, and people to keep him company. He is now raising his third batch of foxhound puppies, who live with him during their summer months on the farm (see page 276 for more on "puppy walking"). Juice is a wonderful addition to our lives. He brings joy to everyone, and he's still cuddly with me and follows me most anywhere. I love him so much. He really is my baby.

Juice and his gang (Gingy and the two foxhound puppies Strangle and Sturdy) make their way around the farm on their evening walk.

Daffodils in the farmyard. Practically the only bulbs we didn't plant!

Another aspect of spring that is so inevitable it seems like a cliché is the daffodils. I thought we had lots of daffodils in America, but in England, they are *everywhere*! People in England get *so excited* by their daffodils. I do love daffodils myself but I am very picky about which ones and where. For the outside, I prefer the ones that are so pale they are almost white, with just a bit of yellow or even that lovely pale orange color on the inside. I also like them in abundance. If you are going to plant daffodils in your garden, you need to really go for it and make a big statement. My mother-in-law has an excellent display herself—there is a large shaded area behind her house, just beyond the lawn, that becomes a huge sea of daffodils come March. She has many varieties and, as a whole, you just can't help but be impressed. As for the typical bright yellow ones that we see everywhere, I favor those cut and arranged in a vase indoors. That intense color is just too much contrast for me in the still-gloomy early-spring landscape. I also love daffodils just before they bloom. As it seems a shame to pick the emerging buds around the farm, I often buy a bunch outside our local food shop to put on the kitchen table. They light up the entire room.

The other yellow flower that emerges in March is the forsythia blossom. I take so much pleasure in clipping a few giant branches and bringing them inside to bloom on the mantelpiece in our sitting room. They look a little gloomy for the first few days—just a bunch of empty twigs—but within a week they are glorious in color and delicate in shape, filling up our whole house with spring joy. I might have two cycles of this and then they are gone, not to return until the next year.

Christopher's birthday falls in March, and we usually mark it with a homemade cake (he *loves* German chocolate, Victoria sponge, and Carrot Cake) and a good long walk—usually on a footpath away from the farm that he has researched in advance, often near some amazing house he wants to show me that is not visible from

Forced forsythia branches brighten up the living room.

The heart-shaped tree on our farm. It looks like this only when the leaves are off it.

any road. The kids always complain—what is it about the concept of a walk that makes kids shudder in horror and revert to their terrible twos? But I have learned to ignore their desperate pleas with the confidence that they most often end up having a good time, maybe even a great one.

We aren't strangers to weekend walks in our family, despite the resistance. Saturdays are always packed with activity, but Sundays usually consist of a leisurely and often quite social lunch, and then an ambitious walk in the fresh air, no matter the weather. At first my kids inevitably resist going out for a long haul, just when they thought they had earned a lazy afternoon, but now they have surrendered to not having a choice, and also to the knowledge that they usually love them as much as we do. They also love the enthusiasm of

Christopher's birthday walk. It must have been an unseasonably warm March day or Zach worked up a sweat while running through the fields.

Ginger, for whom the walk is the highlight of her week, having the whole family out together doing what she loves most. The prospect of an outdoor adventure sends Ginger into a frenzy of excitement, swirling around the yard with her tail tucked under her legs and then her body, jumping so high that all four feet leave the ground. For me, the combination of the wind on my face, the exertion of my body, the occasional company of family and friends, and the chance to get into a casual chat or a meaningful conversation without the distraction of daily life, all make our Sunday walk one of my very favorite things about our life in the country.

Walking during the week on my own—mostly on tracks and paths around the farm—picks up in March as well, and, again, no one loves them more than Ginger. After a few weeks of regular walks, eventually she gets spoiled and thinks that every time I leave the house it means we are going for a walk. Whenever I put on shoes and a coat, she loses her mind with excitement, and it crushes me to disappoint her so often. In March, I love to walk on a certain footpath that leads past a heart-shaped tree, which looks especially so when it is just coming into blossom.

This is the only place on the farm where wild garlic grows, in a shaded area behind Fairgreen House. It first erupts from the ground in March, when I use it to cook with eggs. It is less strong in flavor when boiled or baked. Once the blossoms come out, like here, later in the month or in early April, I use the raw wild garlic to make fresh pesto.

My cooking starts to lighten up in March, moving away from the heavier stews and pies and back in the direction of what's available outside. The first edible plant that grows on the farm in the new season is wild garlic. In late March, it emerges from under a tree in my sister-in-law's backyard. When I first discovered it, I picked it right away and found it to be very, very strong. I've since learned that the earlier you pick it, the stronger it is, so now I try to be patient and wait for it to just start to blossom before I harvest it. Typically, I prefer to use wild garlic for pesto, which I then stir into pasta or drizzle over lamb chops. Because all my enthusiasm for farm produce has been caged over the winter, I get so excited when the wild garlic comes out that I make a huge amount of pesto—enough to pass around liberally on the farm and also to freeze for later when I am craving the taste of early spring.

BAKED EGGS WITH WILD GARLIC
Adapted from Tim Wilson and Fran Warde's
The Ginger Pig: Farmhouse Cookbook

SERVES 1

1 slice good white bread or brioche
Dijon mustard
1 thick slice of bacon, cubed
1 tablespoon wild garlic, shredded (can be
   replaced with chives when unavailable)

1 egg
2 tablespoons heavy cream
freshly ground black pepper
1 tablespoon grated mature hard cheese, such as
   Cheddar, Parmesan, Gruyére, or Comté

Preheat the oven to 350°F. Butter a large ramekin.

Lightly toast the bread, then cut a circle from it that will fit in the bottom of the dish. Spread the toast with a lick of mustard, then place it in the ramekin.

Heat a small frying pan and fry the bacon until crisp. Add the bacon to the ramekin, sprinkle with the wild garlic, then crack an egg on top. Spoon the cream over, add a few twists of pepper, and sprinkle with the cheese.

Bake in the oven for 10–12 minutes, until just firm.

Wild Garlic and Walnut Pesto
Recipe from Hugh Fearnley-Whittingstall

MAKES 4 PORTIONS

3 ounces shelled walnuts
3 ounces wild garlic leaves and stems, washed
  and roughly chopped
1 1/2 ounces Parmesan cheese (or other hard,
  mature cheese), finely grated

zest of 1/2 lemon, finely grated,
  plus a good squeeze of lemon juice
1/2 cup extra-virgin olive oil
sea salt and freshly ground black pepper

Heat the oven to 350°F. Place the nuts in an ovenproof dish and toast for 5–8 minutes, checking from time to time because they burn easily. Remove them from the oven and leave to cool.

Place the toasted nuts in a food processor, along with the wild garlic, Parmesan, and lemon zest. Blitz to a paste, then, with the motor running, slowly add the oil until you have a thick, sloppy purée. Scrape this into a bowl, add a squeeze of lemon, and season to taste. This pesto will keep in a jar in the fridge for a few days. Toss Wild Garlic and Walnut Pesto into hot pasta, swirl it into a vegetable soup, or use it on bruschetta.

CHEESE SOUFFLÉ
From Julia Child's *Mastering the Art of French Cooking*

In spring, I also like to make Cheese Soufflé from my most favorite, special, and coveted cookbook. My neighbor and friend Carole Bamford shares with me a passion for all things Bunny Mellon. The late Bunny Mellon was an American horticulturalist, gardener, philanthropist, and art collector. She also had the best and most refined classic taste in absolutely everything—clothes, flowers, houses, art, food, you name it. When Ms. Mellon's belongings came up for auction at Sotheby's in 2014, Carole and I pored over the catalogs, drooling and overcome with longing. Carole ended up buying her entire cooking library and subsequently gave me Bunny Mellon's own personal copy of Julia Child's *Mastering the Art of French Cooking*. It is no doubt one of the very best gifts I have ever been given. Shortly after, my friend Miranda came to stay, and when I showed her my new most precious object and asked her which recipe we should attempt first (I think I was too intimidated to undertake the task on my own), she looked at me quizzically and responded, "Well, obviously the cheese soufflé," pointing to the recipe that Julia Child was perhaps most famous for, despite being the most difficult to do well. Miranda, having made soufflé before, did all the heavy lifting that first time, but I have since made it all by myself. It's already an English classic, but I also consider it a farm classic.

SERVES 4

Supplies:	Ingredients:
6-cup soufflé mold	*3 tablespoons plus 1 teaspoon salted butter*
2¹/₂-quart saucepan	*³/₄ cup plus 1 tablespoon coarsely grated Swiss, or Swiss*
wooden spoon	*and Parmesan, cheese*
wire whisk	*3 tablespoons white flour*
	1 cup boiling milk
	¹/₂ teaspoon sea salt plus 1 pinch
	¹/₈ teaspoon black pepper
	pinch of cayenne pepper
	pinch of nutmeg
	4 egg yolks
	5 egg whites, total

Preheat the oven to 400°F. Butter the inside of the soufflé mold and sprinkle with the tablespoon of cheese.

Melt the rest of the butter in a 2¹/₂-quart saucepan. Stir in the flour with a wooden spoon and cook over moderate heat until butter and flour foam together for 2 minutes without browning. Remove from heat; when the mixture has stopped bubbling, pour in all the boiling milk at once. Beat vigorously with a whisk until blended. Beat in the ¹/₂ teaspoon of salt and the pepper, cayenne, and nutmeg. Return to moderately high heat and boil, stirring with the whisk, for 1 minute. The sauce will be very thick. Remove from heat.

Immediately start to separate the eggs. Drop the egg white into a separate bowl, and the yolk into the center of the hot sauce. Beat the yolk into the sauce with the whisk. Continue in the same manner with the next 3 eggs. Adjust the seasoning.

Add an extra egg white to the ones in the bowl and beat with a pinch of salt until stiff. Stir a big spoonful (about a quarter of the total) of the egg whites into the sauce. Stir in all but a tablespoon of the cheese. Delicately fold in the rest of the egg whites.

Turn the soufflé mixture into the prepared mold, which should be almost ³/₄ full. Tap the bottom of the mold lightly on the table, and smooth the surface of the soufflé with the flat of a knife. Sprinkle the remaining cheese on top.

Set the mold on a rack in the middle level of the preheated 400°F oven and immediately turn down the heat to 375°F. (Do not open the oven door for 20 minutes.) In 25–30 minutes, the soufflé will have puffed up about 2 inches over the rim of the mold, and the top will be nicely browned. Bake 4–5 minutes more to firm it up, then serve at once.

I serve this with watercress salad simply dressed with extra-virgin olive oil and balsamic glaze.

And finally, March is a time when the plows reappear in the fields around the farm, turning over the soil after a winter's rest and preparing it for fresh planting. Not all the fields will be planted in March and April—some will have been planted already in the autumn and others will be set aside to have a season off, letting nature restore the ground's inherent richness. Seeing the farmers return is always a great sign of optimism for me. Their presence means that the worst of winter is out of the way, the hours of daylight are getting longer, the air is getting warmer, that spring is well on its way.

Spring crocuses, the wonderful result of Christopher's manic, around-the-clock bulb planting.

CHAPTER XI—APRIL

*Awakening of the garden – Planting the raised beds –
Easter – Walking foxhound puppies – Baby animals on the farm –
Managing the chickens*

Somehow in England, we go from what I consider early spring in March directly into "summer" in April. The school term that starts in April is called the *summer term*; the radio announcers start to talk about their favorite things about summer, such as being able to walk their dog without it coming home looking like a swamp thing (okay, I *do* relate to that!); and just a bit later on, Daylesford, our local farmshop, celebrates the height of the season with a summer festival during the third week in May. For me, as an East Coast American, early June is just about when the summer reliably gets going, eventually peaking in July and August. So it took me a while to figure out how the English could consider April, a month when there aren't even leaves on many of the trees, a part of "summer." Perhaps it's based on the reality that there is no reliable "summer" of which to speak in England. Once, we were here visiting from New York at Easter in the end of March and the mercury was over 80 degrees for an entire week. In contrast, many times in my twenty years of farm summers, we have worn sweaters throughout July or been inundated with rain for much of August. What I do notice is that the very peak of lushness and growth does begin at the end of April, picks up a steady pace in May, and culminates with an abundance of fresh green loveliness by the beginning of June. Because the weather is not something to count on, maybe it's the enthusiasm of the garden that defines summer for the Brits? That's my best guess, anyway.

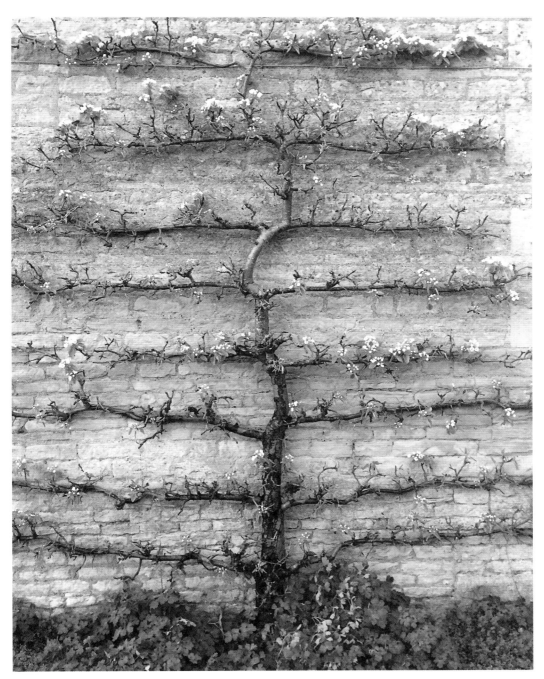

ORCHARDS OF APRIL FLUSH IN SILVER RAIN;
THE CUCKOOS CALL, THE SWALLOWS COME AGAIN.

The big horses—Megan, Sylvie, and Tottie—in the early-spring morning sun. The horses get rotated in the fields around the farm, but when they are in this one, I can often see them from my bedroom window.

Yes, there is reason to celebrate when the garden comes alive—it is incredible!—but most gardens in England possess their beauty year–round, even without the bright colors. What happens in April just before the garden comes alive is, for my sanity, even more important: the sun rises before I do. Not that there is sunlight streaming in my window every morning—this is England, after all—but I don't have that feeling of waking up in the middle of the night when my alarm bell goes off. Just that sliver of light entering the room from behind my drawn velvet curtains makes all the difference in my enthusiasm to start the day, to enter the world.

In April, we take a break from gardening in the flower beds. They have been cleaned and tidied and had their haircuts, so at that point it is just a waiting game. Instead, we turn our attention to the apple orchard, where we have three raised beds for planting fruits and vegetables. You may think three isn't very many, but it's the perfect number for us. And truthfully, we would thrive from produce abundance without planting anything at all in our garden, as both sets of our in-laws have vastly larger kitchen gardens than our own—producing more than we as a whole family could collectively ever consume (leftovers are given to the farmworkers and our neighbors). But how could we live here—in such a fertile, plant-growth-conducive environment—and not grab the opportunity to grow food in our own backyard?

We have tried bringing along umpteen different varieties of fruits and vegetables in our garden on the basis of trial and error. Some things just plain fail, some are ready to be eaten when we are away traveling, some get eaten by caterpillars, and others just produce more than we can possibly eat, leaving us with the guilt of waste. So over the years we have refined our planting down to a pretty minimal and precise science. One whole bed is for strawberries. They thrive, they appear early in the summer when we are reliably at home, and there is nothing better than an indulgent, in situ pig-out. Then there is another whole bed devoted to sweet peas, the ones that never make it into the house. This is my husband's baby. Christopher just stands there in the bed itself, popping open the pods and pouring the raw peas into his mouth. I don't know if it's a childhood habit or just a matter of pure, exquisite flavor for him, but it makes us all happy to watch him enjoy himself so much.

And then the third raised bed is mine. I tend to be more experimental than my husband, although I know that I want a *lot* of rocket (arugula)—it's easy to grow, comes up early in the season, and there is nothing more delicious than a salad (page 61) picked fresh from the soil just minutes before. I have also done well with radishes, rainbow chard, and cauliflower. Nearly everything else I have tried has either died, been gobbled up by insects, or ripened at the wrong time. Clearly this is not your book for vegetable garden advice! But I do enjoy the process immensely, even in such limited quantity. Being a person who is capable of long durations of nearly obsessive focus, I love cleaning out the soil in the beds at the beginning of April—removing rocks, digging up weed roots, and reinforcing the wooden siding. Then I head to my favorite local nursery, where I buy seedlings (I have yet to get my head around growing from seed). It gives me so much satisfaction to lay the plants out in tidy little rows, measuring the recommended distances between them, and finally dig them into the earth. For me, this moment might just be the highlight of vegetable gardening—seeing the soil all raked and smooth with the immaculate lines of young green plants showing so much promise. Then there is harvesting of the actual food we have created and sharing it around the table with friends and family—that just never gets old.

Laying out my veggies in the orchard beds for planting.

April, and more specifically Easter, also brings a farm-to-table meal of another kind—my brother-in-law's home-grown lamb. Although everyone loves the chops or the rack for a good Sunday lunch, we always set aside a sizable leg to roast on Easter Sunday. Having grown up eating my father's own lamb in Virginia (except during those two teenage years when I was on strike), this is a tradition that makes me feel very at home here in England. I even serve the lamb with my father's own Mint Sauce recipe. I have also collected vegetable recipes from here and there—one torn out of a magazine at the hair salon, another from my favorite Ottolenghi cookbook—to make our big Easter lunch my own.

One Easter activity I know I won't give up no matter the kids' age is dyeing eggs. I just love the creativity and unpredictability of it. When I first came to England, I searched high and low for white eggs to dye, but they do not exist here. When I finally surrendered to dyeing brown eggs, I realized what a lovely mellowing effect they have on the dye color and now I always intentionally use brown eggs for dyeing, no matter where I end up for the holiday.

Easter Lunch

Roast Leg of Lamb:

SERVES 6

1 leg spring lamb
olive oil
sea salt and black pepper

12 small sprigs of fresh rosemary
12 garlic slivers
4 marinated anchovy fillets, cut into thirds

I always make lamb the same way. Before covering the leg in olive oil, salt, and pepper, I carve a dozen slits in the skin with a sharp knife and put a rosemary sprig, a sliver of garlic clove, and a third of an anchovy fillet inside each one. (Don't worry, the anchovy doesn't add a fishy taste. It just brings out the lamb flavor, like salt does.) Then I roast the whole thing in a 400°F oven for about 1 hour and 15 minutes, until the inside temperature of the meat reaches 140°F (rare). I love classic Mint Sauce, but this recipe is also good with the Chili and Red Pepper Jam that I make over the winter (see recipe on page 193).

Mint Sauce:

Make this sauce at least two hours before you need it.

YIELDS ENOUGH TO FILL A GRAVY BOAT

*enough mint leaves to fill a cereal bowl
    when stripped from their stems
    and finely chopped*

*3 tablespoons boiling water
3 teaspoons unrefined sugar
4 tablespoons white wine vinegar*

Pour the boiling water over the leaves and leave to infuse. When it is lukewarm, stir in the sugar, then the vinegar, and stir until the sugar has dissolved. Taste and adjust the seasoning before serving.

Roasted Carrots with Dukkah:

I found this recipe in a magazine at the hairdresser.

SERVES 4

2 bunches baby carrots
2 medium red onions, cut into wedges
1 tablespoon dukkah (an Egyptian condiment
consisting of a mixture of herbs,
nuts, and spices—as it has become
popularized recently, you can find it in
most specialty food stores or online)

zest and juice of 1 orange
6 tablespoons olive oil
2 teaspoons red wine vinegar
sea salt and black pepper
2 tablespoons fresh coriander, chopped

Preheat the oven to 350°F. Trim the carrots and place in a large roasting pan with the onion wedges. Toast the dukkah in a small frying pan for 1 minute until browned, and mix with the orange zest and 2 tablespoons of the oil. Drizzle over the carrots and onions and toss well. Roast for 1 hour or until tender.

Mix the remaining oil with the orange juice, vinegar, and a little salt and pepper. Stir into the carrots with the coriander.

Curried Lentils, Potato, and Spinach:

I make this recipe whenever I have leftover potatoes from Sunday lunch.

SERVES 4

1 cup red lentils
4 cups water
1 pound cold roasted potatoes
2 tablespoons canola oil
2 garlic cloves, finely chopped

1 tablespoon curry powder
8 ounces spinach
1 squeeze of lime plus lime wedges, for serving
sea salt and black pepper

Place the lentils in a saucepan with the water and a pinch of salt. Bring to a boil over high heat and then reduce heat to simmer for 15–20 minutes, stirring often with a whisk to help break down the lentils. Add a little more water if it looks too thick.

Cut the potatoes in ¼-inch-thick slices. Heat the oil in a large pan and fry the potatoes for a few minutes. Add the garlic and curry powder and stir. Lower the heat and cook for a minute or two more. Then tip the potatoes into the lentils.

In the same pan used for the potatoes, add the spinach in handfuls, stirring until it wilts. Add the spinach to the lentil and potato mixture. Stir the whole mixture gently, being careful not to break up the potatoes.

Add a good squeeze of lime juice, then season with salt and pepper as desired. Serve right away with lime wedges.

CARROT CAKE WITH GINGER MASCARPONE FROSTING
Adapted from Ina Garten's *Barefoot Contessa Foolproof*

Last Easter Coco took on the task of decorating the carrot cake, to spectacular effect!
Everything she used came from the garden.

My mom gave me my first Ina Garten *Barefoot Contessa* book for Christmas a few years ago, and I've been using it to learn how to bake. I tend to like old-school cake recipes, so I wasn't sure about the Ginger Mascarpone Frosting in lieu of the usual straightforward cream cheese frosting for my Easter Carrot Cake. I also don't love raisins, so I omit them even though the recipe calls for them. This is the best Carrot Cake I have ever eaten, and it has become a unanimous hit with guests as well. I hope you like it as much as we do.

SERVES 8–10

Cake:

2 cups granulated sugar
1 1/3 cups vegetable oil
3 large eggs
1 teaspoon vanilla extract
2 cups plus 1 tablespoon all-purpose flour
2 teaspoons ground cinnamon
2 teaspoons baking soda
1 1/2 teaspoons sea salt
1 pound carrots, grated
1 cup chopped walnuts

Frosting:

12 ounces Italian mascarpone cheese
4 ounces cream cheese
2 cups confectioners' sugar
2 tablespoons heavy cream
1/2 teaspoon vanilla extract
1/3 cup minced crystallized ginger
     (not in syrup)
1/4 teaspoon sea salt

Preheat the oven to 400°F. Grease two round cake pans, line them with parchment paper, and grease again.

Mix together the sugar, oil, and eggs with an electric mixer on medium-high for 2 minutes. Stir in the vanilla. In another bowl, sift together 2 cups of flour, the cinnamon, baking soda, and salt. With the mixer on low, slowly add the dry ingredients to the wet ones.

In a medium bowl, toss together the carrots, walnuts, and 1 tablespoon of flour. Stir into the batter with a rubber spatula. Divide the batter between the two pans and smooth the tops. Bake for 10 minutes, lower the heat to 350°F, and bake for 30–35 minutes more, until an inserted toothpick (or a fork) comes out clean. Cool in the pans for 15 minutes, turn out onto a baking rack, and cool completely.

Meanwhile, make the frosting: With an electric mixer, beat together the mascarpone cheese, cream cheese, confectioners' sugar, cream, and vanilla for about 1 minute, until light and fluffy. Add the crystallized ginger and salt, and beat for 30 seconds more.

Frost the cakes and serve.

As I am writing this book, I am still putting on an Easter egg hunt around the garden for Coco and Zach, ages sixteen and fourteen. This goes back to even before we moved here, as our many spring breaks at the farm often coincided with Easter. I buy loads of foil-wrapped chocolate eggs and hide them in increasingly difficult-to-find places around the yard—in the flower pots, on the limbs of the espaliered pear trees, under the herb bushes, along the fence, and so on. Then for each kid—usually there are four or five, including cousins and houseguests—I hide one very special large golden egg somewhere specific for them just outside the garden—in the orchard or the stables or around the farmyard—and inside is a special present just for them. The whole thing is manic and fun, and we don't seem to be able to give it up quite yet.

The other manic and fun aspect of April is that we receive two eight-week-old foxhound puppies from our local hunt kennels to "walk" for five or six months. Every spring, the foxhound bitches breed new litters, collectively creating too many puppies for the hunt to look after without community support. For the first six months of life, hound puppies need exactly the same things that all puppies do—food, exercise, love, and discipline. So local hunt subscribers volunteer to help raise these little rascals until they are ready to begin training and "enter" the pack. As puppy walking is a local tradition and an essential part of country life, we thought it would be fun to try it out.

Upon receiving our first two hounds—Gadsby and Gallant (named by the hunt, the puppies' names always start with the first two letters of their mother's name, in this case Gaylass)—we realized that the term *puppy walking* was deceptively simple. Having set them up in the stableyard with a straw-lined box of their own, we imagined we'd walk them once or twice a day, and then they'd spend the remainder of their time amusing themselves in the stables and following Ginger around the farmyard. This worked perfectly well for two weeks. They napped for much of the day, spooning each other so sweetly in the stables, until they had enough energy to run around, and then they'd nap again and then run around again. When we walked them around the farm, they would loyally follow Ginger, exploring wherever she explored and following her back to me when I called for them.

The situation seemed manageable and fun. I loved that the hounds made me walk so much, and despite Ginger's initial resistance (in the form of growling) to having to look after two annoying toddlers, it was apparent that she could also see the benefit of getting more walks when they were around. Gadsby and Gallant were the sweetest and funniest little things, but soon they were completely out of control—

Carrying those naughty escape-artist hound puppies home from their latest adventure.

running off on their own, miles away from the farm; following any stranger who walked on the footpath through our farmyard; breaking into our house; jumping over the wall out of their stableyard; and terrorizing my cats. You name the mischief and they got up to it. The first time they disappeared, I was beside myself. I was sure they had run up to the main road and were playing in traffic. I could just imagine myself having to call Michael, the whipper-in (the man whose job it is to look after the hounds), and tell him that I had lost the puppies for good—or worse, that they had come into harm's way. But in fact the hounds had simply run to a local village about two miles away and were being driven around by a local farmer until we ran into him on the road and brought them safely home.

This running off soon became a habit, and we debated every time whether to just lock them up in the stables all day and walk them on leashes, or let them run free, as we had been instructed to do. The thing is, the hounds are meant to learn life's essential lessons by getting into a bit of trouble. They are supposed to get lost and then be able to find their way home. Walking them on leashes—which we tried with little success once or twice—is intuitive for us but absurd for them, as they will never be on a leash once they start their lives as hunting dogs. As for me, I eventually had my own lesson in letting go, slowly learning to trust that the hounds usually made their own way home after going off on an adventure. Gadsby and Gallant ran far and wide around the countryside, and we did receive

Gadsby and Gallant waiting for Gingy on the driveway leading out to the fields.

the occasional call that they had made it to another farm and been locked up there in the stables, or some random car would show up at home with the hounds all giggly and wiggly in the backseat, having been rescued from a nearby road. Word around here spread quickly that we were walking puppies, and the whole community pitched in to alert us to their whereabouts or deliver them safely home when they had strayed too far.

After four months, with an increasingly nagging feeling that the puppies had worn out their welcome in our farmyard and in our community, I started asking the hunt when we were expected to return the hounds to the kennels. Michael simply said, "You'll know when it's time. They will just get too out of control." I did not find this reassuring, as we were supposed to keep them for another month and I was already finding them very difficult to manage. They had found a way to break into our storage room next to the stables and had ripped apart—and ingested!—the stuffing of an entire sofa. Anytime we left the doors to the cottage open, which we often do in summer, they would let themselves in and tear the place up, usually culminating in a nice warm nap on my bed, leaving muddy paw prints all over my sheets.

While the hounds have a wonderful nature, they are not domesticated animals. That becomes apparent over time, and ultimately their wildness keeps you from becoming too attached. Gadsby and Gallant got increasingly aggressive about breaking out of their stables, eventually just jumping over the stone wall. They would run straight for

This is the yard where all the hound puppies live, at least until they grow big enough to jump over the wall.
That's when the dreaded escape action begins.

the house, and, as we'd gotten in the habit of keeping the doors firmly shut, they were like two big bad wolves trying to tear our house down. They jumped and clawed at the windows and doors, scratching the paint and making all kinds of crazy noise and mess. Everyone in the farmyard seemed to lose their goodwill toward them, and soon enough I did as well.

Our first odyssey of babysitting foxhound puppies finally came to an end. I had been bracing myself for the inevitable tears that I thought would come from taking in eight-week-old puppies—loving them, training them, walking them, nurturing them, and very often scolding them—for nearly half a year and then one day sending them off to go live their intended life with the hunt. Why had I set myself up for such heartache? But in the end, I didn't even get to say good-bye to those two naughty boys—the huntsman came to collect them unexpectedly when I was on a trip to New York. And that was okay. I was a bit sad and nostalgic, but also comforted by the knowledge that they are only a couple miles down the road and we can see them when we wish. Mostly, though, I was relieved.

We did go to visit those two troublemakers nearly six months later, when to my surprise, we were considering taking two more puppies for the following summer. Walking foxhounds is like giving birth—you quickly forget the pain and remember only the joy. Also, I suppose I'm still enough of a New Yorker to consider puppy walking an exciting novelty and a fitting contrast to my previous, more urban life. Anyway, we arrived at the kennels and walked over to the yard we were pointed toward. At first I couldn't spot them in the sea of two dozen grown-up hounds, but as soon as I called them, both Gadsby and Gallant came right to the front of the pack and jumped up on the wall to say hi and give us cuddles. I was also a proud mama to hear that they were among the best trained when they returned from our care and were the first two to be "coupled" with an older hound to be taught the ways of the pack.

In early summer the following year, we received an invitation from the hunt to attend their annual puppy show, which would include our babies, Gadsby and Gallant. As walkers, we got special privileges, like being invited to the rehearsals and going to a formal lunch on the day of the show. I drove over to the first rehearsal with my mother-in-law, who explained to me on the way there how the whole thing worked. All the new puppies that the hunt had elected to keep (they sell those they don't want to other hunts) are presented to two judges—usually the huntsman or master from another hunt—in pairs. Hound dogs first, bitches second. The whippers-in wear white lablike coats and black bowler hats.

It's all very old-school and chic. The judges wear navy pin-striped suits and bowler hats. Also chic. In fact, the whole thing is stylish—the kennels, the mannerisms, the tradition, the formality—but the event in and of itself is really just a folly. The judges analyze the hounds' conformation, their behavior, and their attitude. The top eight are then selected to go for a "gallop" in the field for further assessment. After that, the top six are given places and trophies.

In the rehearsals I went to, Gadsby and Gallant did terribly. Neither of them made it to the "gallop" phase in any of the three rehearsals I saw. At the last rehearsal, however, one of the masters told me that Gadsby had not only made it to the "gallop" but had come fourth overall. So I had some hope that in the puppy show Gadsby at least had a chance. Sad as it is to say, Gallant never showed much promise, which wasn't a big surprise to me. Whenever we had taken him out for a walk on our farm, he would lag behind and get distracted easily, and almost never came when he was called. In any case, despite our enthusiasm and a small amount of hope, Gadsby was the second hound eliminated on the big day, right after Gallant, who was the first. Gadsby had a kind of self-satisfied smile on his face as he was carried out of the ring that day. He's a character. Anyway, despite our lack of success, we were given twin silver teaspoons with our puppies' names and the monogram of the hunt engraved on them as a thank-you for our puppy-walking generosity, and we went home feeling proud to have seen our babies graduate from puppies to fully grown hounds.

The latest batch of hounds we walked were a bitch, Challice, and a hound, Chanter. This time we warned our neighbors in advance of the upcoming mayhem, but these two didn't run away nearly as often as Gadsby and Gallant. What they did excel at, however, was escaping much earlier and much more successfully from the yard where they lived. Challice was especially good at jumping both the metal gate and the stone wall; and when we blocked those off, she managed to jump the even taller wooden fence into the stableyards and then slipped through a ten-by-ten-inch-hole in the big gate intended to keep the horses contained. We tried closing it off with string and tape, but Challice just chewed right through it. She was a total cat burglar. When my sister-in-law complained that they were making their way into her house and creating a giant mess, we had to surrender, and we sent the puppies back to the kennels a month ahead of schedule.

As I am writing this book, we are walking our third set of hound puppies, two bitches called Sturdy and Strangle. Personality-wise, they are my favorite ones we've had—so far mostly possessing the best qualities of our previous hounds with less of the worst ones. Long may it last!

Top: Challice and Chanter giving Gingy a run for her money. The months when the hound puppies are with us are Ginger's most in-shape time of the year. Above: Kisses for Strangle and Sturdy on a mid-walk break.

Hound puppies aren't the only babies around in April. Since we moved here to the farm we have had, at various times, five Kunekune pigs, two Gloucestershire Old Spot pigs, two bunnies, two donkeys, countless chickens, about a dozen horses, including two foals, and a slew of lambs all born in and around the April birthing season. The set of Kunekune triplets adopted by my brother-in-law arrived on a particularly cold late-April day. They were driven into a field by a pickup truck with the cages loaded on the back. As soon as we were allowed to open up the metal doors, we took them in our arms and cuddled them. Delicious! We all took turns holding and cuddling the piglets and taking our picture with them. It was a short-lived pleasure, though, as within just a few weeks they were already too heavy to lift and too independent to seek human affection. They have always remained incredibly friendly toward us, however, running toward us and squealing whenever we approach their field. Sometimes we bring fallen apples from the orchard to feed them, and they sit and beg when you hold the apple close to their mouth. It's hilarious.

The three little piggies. They were so sweet. When I walked by their field, they all ran over to the fence to say hello and get their backs stroked. I have found that all pigs love affection. When you give it to them, a look of joy is tangible on their faces.

Clockwise from top: Clementine, one of a set of twin pigs Coco received for her tenth birthday; Jack Bauer and Inspector Clouseau checking out what's going on in the next field; little newborn Packer Moose standing protected by her mother, Megan.

*Clockwise from top left: Three newborn lambs following their mother for milk; Padmé, Zach's bunny, as a baby—
she still looks pretty much the same; a Bantam hen and four of her babies staying nearby her to keep warm.
As you can see, some were still left to hatch.*

It took us a while to get our chicken-hatching program going. The first year we decided to breed and raise our own fuzzy little yellow and black chicks, our plans were thwarted by a sneaky fox who got into the chickenhouse one night and ate our beloved rooster, Kaiser. He was a glorious boy, with a rich red comb and slick black-and-green iridescent tail feathers. We had raised him from a baby, and he was just coming into his own, strutting around the farmyard like he owned the place. I'm pretty sure he died defending the seven "ladies," who were his roommates in the coop. What a hero! We have since learned our lesson, and our chickens now live in a much less romantic, but much more protected, enclosure. They no longer roam free around the farmyard, congregating on the garden bench outside my kitchen window to say hello to me every morning, but we haven't had a chicken swiped by a fox in three years, so it is well worth it. Our chicken-rearing skills, however, have only increased marginally. Our hens appear to be determinedly unbroody, so all our eggs end up in an incubator. Some never hatch and others hatch but die quickly.

We've had a few successes, most notably Chatty Cathy. An extremely talkative girl, she was the only chick in her brood to survive, so we decided to raise her in the house. Cathy was such a good cuddler. Every time we settled into the TV room after dinner, she would come right over to the closest warm body—even if that meant Ginger!—and snuggle right up. She particularly liked nuzzling in right under Christopher's chin and staying there for a long time. Hours, actually. Once she outgrew her cage, she moved into the stables for a while and befriended our groom Sinead's dog, Elffy. Elffy and Cathy bonded quickly and became devoted friends. In that period, Cathy definitely identified as a dog. She loved it when Elffy chased her around the stableyard, and they would roll and wrestle around just like two puppies. But then one day we realized that Cathy was going to need to become a chicken at long last. So we slowly introduced her to the other hens and she is now well integrated. Unlike the others, however, when we enter their yard, Cathy runs straight over to us and is happy to be picked up for a hug and kiss. What a sweet girl. Except that it turns out she's not a girl . . . Our sweet little Cathy grew into a rooster!

For new life, new growth, and the hope of better weather, April is a promising and joyful month in the life of most farms, not excluding this one.

Opposite, top: In our free-range days, every time a rooster got eaten by a fox, I kept a feather from his body (at least when the fox left anything behind) as a memento. They sit on the windowsill in my bedroom.

Opposite, bottom: I loved it when the hens hung out on the bench outside my kitchen window all day.

This page, top: I love the romance of free-roaming chickens, but nothing kills that joy like a hungry fox.

This page, bottom: Cathy, our beloved home-raised chick.

The new home of all the chickens (and a few bunnies). Since we have them living in the yard we haven't had a fox attack in three years.

CHAPTER XII—MAY

Swallows – Espaliered pears – Oilseed rape – Blossoms in the orchard – Cow parsley along the drive – Bluebells in the woods – Raising foals – My birthday – Summer meals – Raising our children – Benefits of farm life

MAY is a transformational time on the farm. We go from heavy suggestions of spring at the beginning of the month—a mixture of fresh green and leftover winter brown—to a lush expression of early summer. Blossoms, flowers, and a full spectrum of emerald green cover the landscape by the end of the month.

As far as Christopher is concerned, the arrival of swallows back at the farm marks the beginning of the summer. Swallows are migratory birds that spend each winter all the way in South Africa and then make the journey, pretty much nonstop (literally sleeping while they fly!), each year back to the place where they were born. Our farm, and more specifically our farmyard, is the birthplace of many swallows. Of the hundred or so that leave in October, typically only thirty or forty make it back the following May, and when they arrive home again, they set about trying to produce offspring to replenish their numbers. A female typically can produce two sets of hatchlings in a summer. The swallows are the great athletes of the bird world, and they seem to take delight in their ability to perform elaborate acrobatics. They survive off insects, which they take on the wing rather than forage on the ground. Christopher is particularly fascinated by the life cycle and migration of the swallows and watches closely for the arrival, breeding habits, procreation success, and departure each year.

GOLDEN AND AZURE, GREEN AND WHITE IS MAY;
BUTTERCUPS, BLUEBELLS, FERNS, AND HAWTHORN SPRAY.

January

February

March

July

August

September

Our cottage garden lights up with apple blossoms around midmonth—such beautiful and promising pale pink blooms—but my favorite are the white pear blossoms on our espaliered trees at the end of the house. Christopher planted and trained them more than twenty years ago, and they *make* our house, as far as I am concerned. At any time of the year, you can stand in front of the pear trees and know

April

May

June

October

November

December

what month it is depending on what they are doing—leaves, no leaves, the size of the fruit, the first sign of buds, the stark branches of January—but there is nothing more satisfying than the few weeks when the perfectly aligned and pruned branches come to life with such delicate and vibrant green leaves and white flowers. It might just be one of the prettiest displays of nature on the whole farm.

The oilseed rape blossoms in the field along our driveway where the three big oak trees and a giant willow all stand tall in the landscape.

In May we also get the vivid yellow oilseed rape (an indelicate name for such a pretty crop!) blossoms out in the fields. Entire crops become solid shapes of electric sunny color due to the intensity and proximity of their flowers, and not just on our farm but all around Oxfordshire. Green fields are checkered with yellow ones, making for spectacular views all around the countryside. They remind me of something you'd more likely see in France or Belgium than in England, but I'm not complaining! The blossoms have also been a nice reward for moving here, as I was never here in May until we came full time, so I had no idea this occurred. Oilseed rape, I have since learned, is a major crop in our part of the world. On our farm, the farmers sell the beans that grow out of the blossoms for cattle feed. In addition, a local cottage industry has grown out of making rapeseed oil, which is the same as what we Americans call *canola oil*. Go to any local farmers' market around here and you'll find young farmers selling it and making anything they can think of from it. Because crops are rotated every year, the great big splash of yellow turns up in different places from year to year. I often don't notice whether a field is wheat or corn or rape until May, when the plant itself becomes more defined and obvious. In some years, the yellow fields surround our house, while in others they might surround the bridle path where I ride, or the driveway, or my favorite walk in the woods. Wherever they appear, they are gorgeous.

The other magical plant that pops up all around the farm and the surrounding countryside in May is what Americans call *Queen Anne's lace* and the English call *cow parsley*. The collective effect of these lacy off-white flowers and their feathery foliage along the roads, in the unfarmed fields, and in front of hedges along the drive, frames the entire landscape in a romantic soft focus. The month of cow parsley's presence in England gets me every single time and is arguably the most beautiful of the year.

In the spring when the blossoms are fully flared and the sun sets later in the day is my favorite time to soak in the hot tub before bed.

In case that isn't enough gushing about the beauty of the English countryside in May, there's one more absolute stunner: bluebells. I first discovered them when I was riding my horse Shalom down on the bottom of the farm alongside a wood belonging to our neighbors. As we strode past an opening in the trees, I noticed an intense purple glow coming from the bottom of the forest. It was truly an entire carpet of blossoms spread out across the earth under the surrounding trees, and it was spectacular. Each year since, we make a point of returning to that same wood, either on horseback or on foot, with Ginger and the kids in tow, to have a picnic and savor the bluebell moment.

May is the month when most of the racehorse foals belonging to my brother-in-law and mother-in-law are born. On average, we have a foal on the farm every couple of years, and it's always so exciting when we do. For a while there was a mare named Crimson who was in foal (preggers!) three years in a row before we eventually retired her from breeding. She produced a colt named Felix, who went on to become a decent racehorse. I remember so well one summer seeing Coco sit on top of the five-bar gate at the field entrance watching something very intently. She must have been about seven or eight. I wandered over to see what was captivating her, and it was her uncle, starting to work on taming Felix. He was down on his hands and knees in the field, making himself smaller than the foal, trying to get him to approach. After a while, Coco's uncle called her over to help him. He gave lots of love and affection to Crimson so that she wouldn't become aggressive in protecting her baby, and Coco crouched down low and waited until Felix came to check her out, which he eventually did do. He sniffed the top of her head and let her reach up to gently touch his nose. It was the sweetest moment and one that has stayed with both Coco and me ever since.

More recently, PackerMoose (a combination of names suggested by young cousins), a filly foal, was born in 2014. There was no need to tame her, as she grew up with us handling her since day one. Anticipation of her arrival was high from the day we found out her mother, Megan, was in foal. Megan is a great hunter and exceptional jumper (she won the Heythrop Hunt gate-jumping competition in 2014, jumping more than six feet), but she tends to be a little slow on the flat. So my brother-in-law had the idea that he would breed her with a thoroughbred to add in some speed, with the hope that the resulting horse would be a great eventer one day. We waited eleven long months for little PackerMoose to arrive, and when she did—in the second week of May—we were all elated for days afterward. I had never seen a day-old horse for myself, nor had the kids. She was cute beyond belief! At ten days old, she returned home to our farm from another farm nearby that is essentially a maternity center for local horses—considering

Young Coco crouched down on her knees in the field to make herself more approachable to baby Felix.

the money at stake with racehorses, you don't want to risk any complications, nor do you want to stand next to the knocked-up horse for weeks, waiting for it to give birth. Watching little PackerMoose grow up on the farm was one of the most gratifying experiences we have all had since moving here. We spent hours in the field with her—she would lie down next to us with her head in our laps, she would jump up and rest her front hooves on our shoulders, she would do her clumsy first canter with a leg or two kicking out to the side with excitement. She loved us, and we loved her.

I was filled with dread at the thought of PackerMoose being weaned from Megan. The plan was to put our resident nanny, Sailor, a thirty-year-old pony who is rarely ridden but whom all the horses seem to love, in the field with mother and baby. That way, PackerMoose would get used to her new companion so that when separated from her mother, she would at least have a new friend with whom she was already acquainted. Two weeks later, the day before Megan and PackerMoose were to be separated, I walked by the field and saw that, instead of the two of them standing together as usual, Megan was trying to run away from her foal. Every time PackerMoose approached her mother, Megan would run off. Seeing that the natural weaning process had already begun, I felt better about the pending separation. The next day, we put PackerMoose and Sailor together in a stable while Megan was loaded onto a horse box to leave the farm for a little while. She would

start the long road back to fitness at a nearby farm while giving her foal some space to adapt to life without her. Megan seemed absolutely fine, but despite Sailor being right there with her, PackerMoose was shaking all over and her eyes were wild. She whinnied and whinnied, and I stayed there with her for a while until she seemed to calm down a bit. It wasn't easy, but it wasn't totally heartbreaking, either. I felt that we'd done all we could to make the process as gentle as possible, and she was in good hands with Sailor. Within forty-eight hours, she and Sailor went back in the field and life went on. A month later, my brother-in-law got a thoroughbred foal from France named Jimmy—same age as Moose—so they could keep each other company while they ate and grew and eventually were broken. They are now both about to turn three. Jimmy has been sold as a potential racehorse, and Moose has been broken and is training to be an eventing horse. And Christopher's hunter Sylvie, who is out with an injury for the coming year, is currently in foal, sired by William Fox-Pitt's eventer Chilli Morning, on whom he won the Badminton Horse Trials. And so the horse-breeding cycle on Fairgreen Farm begins again.

PackerMoose grew up to be the sweetest mare we've ever had on the farm. You can hug her neck, kiss her nose, and stroke her face, and she holds perfectly still, enjoying the affection. I suspect it's because she was handled so much at such a young age. On our farm, when we like a horse's personality, we say she's "a really nice person," which is different from being good to ride. Polo, for example, is fantastic and gentle to ride, but he's not a very nice person. He bullies the other horses.

My own birthday is in May as well—the thirteenth. (And yes, sometimes it falls on a Friday.) Since having kids, I tend to put my attention on their birthdays instead of mine, but I've had a few great ones here as well. The most memorable was my fortieth. Christopher and I dropped the kids at school and then jumped on the train headed up to London. By eleven a.m., we were on Lamb's Conduit Street at a tailor shop, having a tweed hacking jacket custom-made for me—my present from Christopher. The shop was called Connock & Lockie—an old-school tailor specializing specifically in tweed—that had recently been taken over by a talented and fashion-relevant twenty-six-year-old Japanese kid, Yusuke Nagashima. After having my measurements taken and choosing the fabric—a charcoal-gray-and-black herringbone from Harris Tweed—Christopher and I made our way down the street to a delicious lunch at a Spanish restaurant, Cigala, that we'd always wanted to try. It did not disappoint. After that, we got back on the train headed home, swooped up the kids from school, picked up my mother-in-law from home, and went to the sister pub of our local—it's called the Wheatsheaf. It's a little farther away and a bit more formal, which made it feel like a special occasion. That day was pretty much a perfect birthday, and I cherished it because birthdays are complicated and they don't always feel good or meet expectations, do they?

Even though the outdoors is so utterly gorgeous around here in May, the inside of the house gets its share of attention too. In May, I take the heavy flannel sheets and wool blankets off the beds and replace them with my favorite vintage linen ones, covered with much lighter duvets. I also take all the houseplants—mostly scented geraniums, Chinese money plants, and jade—outside for some direct sun, rainwater, and fresh air. I carry all my heavy winter sweaters, jackets, and boots out to be stored in the barn and return to the cottage with more cheerful summer dresses, flowing skirts, and open-toe shoes. The kitchen gets a tidy-up as well. I get rid of all the old condiment jars in the pantry, reorganize drawers, sort through forgotten things in the freezer, and take note of what I have to tell my husband to *please* stop buying. He has a compulsive habit of stocking up on English mustard, mint jelly, and mango chutney—we must have half a dozen bottles of each at any one time. Our little pantry has no room for such excess!

With the kitchen shipshape, I get down to some serious summer cooking, inspired by all that is growing on our farm or on the surrounding ones. May is a month in which the entire country seems to collectively celebrate the arrival of asparagus. You can grow your own asparagus, buy the posh version in a posh farmshop, or simply pick it up at your local grocery. Frankly, I have found that it doesn't really matter because, apart from the undeniable satisfaction in growing

My favorite corner of the living room, where I'm surrounded on one side by lovely houseplants and sunshine and on the other side by the fireplace. Fatboy and I are usually in competition for the red chair. He won that day.

The bounty from a typical trip to our nearest food shop usually looks like this, fresh and local produce wrapped up in recycled packaging. It's such a pleasure to buy my groceries there.

your own food, for the most part it all tastes the same. Here, fresh produce tastes like fresh produce regardless of where you buy it. And one thing that impresses me about England is that when a fruit or vegetable is in season, it is farm-fresh no matter where you buy it. Strawberries, raspberries, rhubarb, potatoes, cauliflower, and, yes, asparagus are among the produce that is local to our area and better than any I can remember having tasted anywhere in America.

With the asparagus, my easy, lazy option is simply trimming them, steaming them, and then dipping them into four-and-a-half-minute soft-boiled eggs with a little Maldon sea salt and pepper. You can't beat the ease or satisfaction when two such basic ingredients come together so simply and successfully.

If I am feeling more ambitious with the asparagus, I will take on a risotto. The first few recipes I tried were unremarkable, so much so that I thought, "Maybe I've just gone off risotto?" Determined to try again, I went to my quite extensive cookbook shelf to find an authority on the recipe. I flipped through one or two books that looked promising and either didn't find a recipe or found one that had some unconventional ingredient that turned me off. I tend to always like the simplest and most classic version of any recipe. And then I remembered the *Silver Spoon* cookbook. I bought it a year ago at the urging of an Italian friend who declared it to be the bible of every Italian housewife. How could I resist that endorsement? But when it arrived, I found it overwhelming—too comprehensive, too thick to flip through, and practically too heavy to lift off the shelf! So it just sat there until I was in search of my Asparagus Risotto recipe. My eye landed on the thick volume, and I thought—"Ah! This must be it." And it was. I glanced at the recipe (in the midst of every other traditional Italian recipe for risotto that was ever invented) and saw that it was simple and straightforward—the whole thing, ingredients included, only took up a quarter of a page! I made it in mid-May on a rare night that I was home alone, thinking I'd treat myself to cooking something ambitious, just for me. I knew things were headed in a good direction when I tasted one of the asparagus tips I'd been instructed to sauté in butter before adding to the rice. I could have just stopped there and inhaled every one of them, perfectly satisfied. But I persevered, and when I finished with a squeeze of lemon over the top, I poured myself a glass of Sancerre and sat down in the living room with Gingy by my side to relax and enjoy my meal by the fire (yes, a fire in May!). I wondered if the risotto tasted so good because I was undistracted by friends or family chatting away next to me, or because I was *really* hungry. But I have now made this recipe many times since—especially for vegetarian Coco—and each time it impresses me again. I have definitely *not* gone off risotto!

STEAMED ASPARAGUS AND SOFT-BOILED EGGS

SERVES 1

4 asparagus stalks
2 eggs
sea salt and black pepper

Bring two small pots of water to a boil. Snap the ends off the asparagus and set aside. With a spoon, carefully lower two room-temperature eggs (I never store mine in the fridge) into one of the pots of boiling water. Boil the eggs for four and a half minutes.

While the eggs are cooking, place the asparagus spears into the other pot of boiling water. Watch carefully: as soon as they start to brighten in color, remove them and run under cold water to stop the cooking process. Nothing worse than soggy asparagus!

Remove one egg at a time with a slotted spoon and hold it in your hand with a tea towel to guard against the heat. Tap a very sharp knife two-thirds of the way up the egg to chop off the top. Season with salt and pepper. Dip your asparagus stalks into the gooey egg yolk and then eat the rest of the egg with a small spoon. The key is to eat the eggs while they are piping hot. Luke-warm egg yolk is not very nice.

ASPARAGUS RISOTTO
Adapted from Clelia D'Onofrio's *The Silver Spoon*

SERVES 4

1 pound, 2 ounces asparagus, spears trimmed
6 ¼ cups vegetable stock
5 tablespoons salted butter
3 tablespoons olive oil

½ medium onion, chopped
2 cups arborio rice
sea salt
Parmesan cheese, freshly grated, for serving

Cook the asparagus in a pot of salted, boiling water for 10–12 minutes until tender, then drain and cut off and reserve the spears. Chop the stems and set aside.

Bring the vegetable stock to a boil.

Meanwhile, melt 1 tablespoon butter in a skillet, add the asparagus spears, and cook over low heat, stirring occasionally, for 5 minutes, then remove from heat and set aside.

Melt 2 tablespoons of butter with the olive oil in a pan, add onion, and cook over low heat, stirring occasionally, for 5 minutes.

Stir in the rice and cook, stirring, until the grains are coated in fat, then add the chopped asparagus stems.

Add a ladleful of the hot stock and cook, stirring, until it has been absorbed. Continue adding the stock, a ladleful at a time, and stirring until it has been absorbed. This will take 18–20 minutes.

When the rice is tender, stir in the remaining butter and the asparagus spears.

Serve with grated Parmesan.

Of course, these quiet evenings to myself are few and far between, but much appreciated on the occasions when they occur. One of the ways in which I have most enjoyed our family life on the farm is having a more balanced division of parental duties with Christopher. It has to be said that Christopher has always been a relatively hands-on, heavily participatory dad, but on the farm he's even more so. We run the house, the farm, the animals, and the kids together as a team. We take turns going to the kids' sports matches, doctor's appointments, and teacher meetings, and we try our best to follow the "I cook, so you clean up" rule. That one works quite well, although I have a much more comprehensive and specific idea of what a clean kitchen should look like. But still, the effort is much appreciated.

From a child-rearing perspective, one of the reasons Christopher and I feel so grateful to have made the move to the English countryside is that we feel we bought the kids another year or two of childhood. When we left New York City, Coco was nearly eleven, the only girl in her year at school not to have a phone, and she was asking for grown-up items of clothing like fluorescent pink cut-off shorts from Abercrombie & Fitch that nearly showed the bottoms of her butt cheeks. One month into our new life in England and wanting desperately to fit into her more innocent, wholesome surroundings, Coco was dressed head to toe in more age-appropriate Jack Wills clothes and Cath Kidston accessories. Zach has also thrived in his new life, albeit more reluctantly. He discovered a great passion for the classics, specifically Greek mythology and Latin language, two subjects often not covered in American schools. Also, he was required to not only do PE but also play on a sports team every term of the year. Zach has very little inclination in sports and would have gotten away with the bare minimum in New York. But here, there is a team for every level of player in rugby, hockey, football (soccer to us Americans), and cricket, and Zach has received the many benefits of learning to be a team player and excelling in areas where he previously had no interest, slowly disproving his theory that he had minimal talent. In fact, he has discovered that he is quite a good rugby player. At school, both kids had required nature class (learning the names of local trees, flowers, birds, and the like), spent their recess climbing the horse chestnuts and beeches, and were required to shake hands and make eye contact with their headmaster on the way in and out of school every day. Immediately, their manners improved immensely. The English have hands-down the best manners in any culture I have ever encountered, and the reinforcement of this at home, in school, and in their peer group made a big impact on them very quickly. I am so proud of how polite both my children have become.

Now with both Coco and Zach at boarding school with many kids from London and from countries around the world, they have become global citizens again.

*Christopher and the kids on an evening stroll around the farm. I'm there, too, but behind the camera as usual.
Our family walks create some of my favorite moments on the farm.*

However, they have a stronger sense of who they are and a greater depth of maturity with much thanks to their diverse upbringing. It's fun to watch them interact with friends from all over the world and incorporate all they have learned from the varying totality of their lives. In the end, both my children will have had plenty of time on the farm and in the English countryside to have it be a core foundation of their formative years, the results of which, however, have been quite different in each child.

Very shortly after we arrived in England, I had an epiphany about Coco. It was as if I suddenly understood her in a whole new way. I observed her natural ease in her more rural surroundings, her easy assimilation into this new, more reserved culture, and her immediate acquisition of a perfect English accent, and suddenly her whole being came into sharper focus for me. Simply put, she's English. She just *is* and always has been, naturally, English. In sharp contrast, Zach has become almost defiantly more American in many ways. Like me, he just *is* American. Despite moving here at a younger and more impressionable age than Coco, his accent hasn't become any less Yankee since the day we moved here. His friendly, affectionate, outgoing personality has stayed with him as well. So despite both my children emphasizing one aspect of their life over the other, I feel they have both gotten the full benefits of their city and country, American and English lives, and for that I am grateful.

May is also the kickoff of our humble kitchen garden in the orchard, beginning with rhubarb. Rhubarb seems to be the garden's greatest gift, with stalks regrowing throughout the summer. If there is one recipe I am most known for both on the farm and within our group of countryside friends, it is my Rhubarb Crumble. Diane von Furstenberg used to say to me, "Every woman needs to be known for something, even if it's for making the best apple pie." Well, I took that to heart quite literally and have made sure that everyone I care about gets to share in my love of Rhubarb Crumble.

It began when Christopher planted rhubarb in the orchard beside our house. I was so excited to see those gorgeous pink-and-green stalks emerge from the ground, but I had no idea what to do with them. I have always been sort of bummed out when someone serves stewed rhubarb—or any kind of stewed fruit—for dessert. If I'm going to send my glucose levels soaring, it's going to have to include butter and flour to be worth it.

I first tried a few crumble recipes I found on the Internet—finding them too fruity, or too sweet (if rhubarb can ever be called that), or too mushy. And then I discovered Rose Elliot's version in *The Guardian*. I halved the sugar that is stirred into the fruit and skipped the wholemeal flour in favor of good old all-purpose flour. My version has been a hit again and again—the tanginess of the rhubarb softened by the crispy, buttery, just-sweet-enough crumble top. My family demands it at nearly every festive summer meal, and my friends sometimes call before joining us for a dinner party to make sure it's on the menu.

Speaking of DVF, her personal chef, Jane Coxwell, has a wonderful cookbook called *Fresh Happy Tasty*, which I use a ton in everyday life, and her Poached Rhubarb with Vanilla Bean, Ginger, and Cardamom is also one of my favorite rhubarb recipes, which I know sounds like a contradiction to what I said in the previous paragraph. But what I discovered is that while I don't love stewed fruit as a dessert, I do like it for breakfast. She suggests serving it over sheep's yogurt, which is exactly what I do throughout much of the summer, and it couldn't be more delicious.

RHUBARB CRUMBLE

SERVES 8

Fruit:

2 pounds rhubarb
3 tablespoons caster sugar

Crumble:

1³/₄ cups all-purpose flour
2 teaspoons baking powder
1¹/₃ cups soft salted butter or margarine
(I use Lurpak Spreadable butter)
1¹/₃ cups demerara sugar

Preheat the oven to 400°F. Trim the rhubarb and cut it into 1¹/₂-inch pieces. Place in a shallow oval baking dish (see the photo of the one I use). Sprinkle the caster sugar over the fruit.

For the crumble, sift the flour and baking powder into a mixing bowl. Add the butter and massage it in with your fingers until the mixture looks like bread crumbs. Mix in the sugar. Pour the crumble over the rhubarb, making sure it covers the fruit mixture completely.

Bake for 25–30 minutes, until the top is crisp and golden brown and the rhubarb tender. Serve with heavy cream or crème fraîche. Or nothing. I like it on its own.

POACHED RHUBARB WITH
VANILLA BEAN, GINGER, AND CARDAMOM
Adapted from Jane Coxwell's *Fresh Happy Tasty*

SERVES 2

1 1/2 cups agave nectar
1 vanilla bean, split lengthwise and seeds
    scraped out
1/4-inch piece fresh ginger, peeled
1 cardamom pod
thin strips lemon zest, each about 1 inch

4 cups water
1/2 pound rhubarb stalks, cut into
    4-inch pieces
sheep's milk yogurt, or other plain yogurt,
    for serving

Combine the agave nectar, vanilla pod and seeds, ginger, cardamom, and lemon zest in a medium saucepan with water and bring to a boil over medium-high heat. Immediately reduce heat to low and simmer for 10 minutes.

Add the rhubarb and simmer for 3–5 minutes until tender, depending on the size of the rhubarb. Be careful not to overcook or boil, or the rhubarb will lose its shape and fall apart.

Remove the pan from heat and set aside to cool. Serve over yogurt.

Cold Chicken with Parsley Jelly
From Ambrose Heath's *Herbs in the Kitchen*

Lately I've gotten into researching the history of country life in England in hopes of discovering and recovering some lost traditions. There are a great many books I have discovered, mostly thanks to the amazing Bodleian Library at Oxford. I found one or two old country life books—about houses, gardens, food, hobbies, sports, clothes, or any relevant topic, really—and

then I searched online for a copy to buy. In many cases I learned that the books are one of many in a series and I spent hours tracking down a complete set. To understand the new culture in which I live, and understand how it came to be and the influences that ultimately defined it, helps me to take greater ownership of my new life here. I have also found some wonderful recipes, like Cold Chicken with Parsley Jelly (had never heard of that before, have you?), which is a perfect summer lunch or dinner. I have also found inspiration for Christmas decorations found in nature (old-man's-beard!), vintage hunting clothes to search for on eBay, new flowers to grow in the garden, pottery, ceramics, interiors, illustrations, you name it!

Fills six 8-ounce jars
Parsley Jelly:
fresh parsley leaves
1 lemon
1 pound granulated sugar

Fill a saucepan with parsley leaves and barely cover them with cold water. Bring to a boil and gently simmer for half an hour. Then measure the liquid and add the juice of a large lemon and its rind for every pint. Strain, measure again, and allow a pound of granulated sugar to each pint of the liquid. Boil until the jelly sets, and pot in small jars, covering them when cold.

   Serve with cold leftover roast chicken.

By the last week in May, I look outside and realize that this is the time of year that is most important to savor. I make a conscious decision to take a moment each day to really look at and appreciate the flowers blooming in the garden, the trees glowing in their fresh green glory, the baby animals getting acquainted with life in the fields, the fruit and vegetables poking their heads up from the soil. After a few weeks, it's impossible not to take some of these pleasures for granted, but May is the time when you feel like you've arrived at the moment you've been waiting for during the darker winter months and there is still enough time to feel as though good times are ahead for quite a while.

What I have found is that who you are follows you wherever you go. I am a person who thrives on evolution and personal growth. Making a dramatic life change has suited me well, as has living a much simpler, more focused life, but it has not been without its growing pains. I am not immune to periods of moodiness, questioning, and restlessness. I can have the most idyllic day—pick fresh figs from the garden for breakfast, bottle-feed a baby lamb, ride my horse, cook a delicious meal for lunch or dinner, have hours of uninterrupted writing time in my office, read my book in the bath before falling asleep—and it's not always a guarantee that I am going to feel happy. Farm life is more wonderful than anything else when it feels wonderful, but it hasn't made me exempt from inevitable highs and lows, and everyday worries and anxieties. What it has done is provide a structure and a lifestyle that promotes greater and more frequent happiness, and the consistency of this life has given me a more thorough sense of myself and how to manage the normal fluctuation of joys and challenges, inspiration and boredom, happiness and sadness.

If only Juice and I were walking off into the sunset together. He would love that. I probably would too.

Photo Credits

Title page (right), 248: Coco Brooks

Pages 15, 23, 40–41, 42, 43, 44–45, 46–47, 62–63, 65, 69, 70, 113 (top right), 203, 210, 303: Oberto Gili

Pages 19, 25, 30–31, 37 (bottom right), 66–67, 68, 92–93: The Selby

Pages 22, 29, 32, 33 (both), 80, 130, 131, 208, 244: Courtesy the Brooks family

Pages 54, 147, 157, 213, 220, 277, 283 (bottom), 300–301, 315: Christopher Brooks

Pages 102–103: Bastien Halard

Page 125: Chris Floyd

Page 134: Zachary Brooks

Page 176: Sinead Logush

Page 191: Pamela Hanson

Aknowledgments

THANK YOU, Richard Pandiscio, David Kuhn, William LoTurco, Kate Mack, David Rosenthal, Kate Napolitano, Jason Booher, Rebecca Strobel, Stephanie Kelly, John Parsley, Chris Floyd, Miranda Brooks, Nancy Meyers, Jessica Seinfeld, Jeremy Clarkson, Amy Astley, Regena Thomashauer, Christy Powell, Rebekah Brooks, Charlie Brooks, Caroline Brooks, Annabel Brooks, Oberto Gili, Todd Selby, Pamela Hanson, Camilla Harrison, Fay Dyer, Tomak Ciura, Sinead Logush, and Richard Fudge.

With SPECIAL THANKS to Sarah Hochman and Bill Loccisano, my closest collaborators, who worked tirelessly and patiently, yet again, on my behalf.

And, finally, THANK YOU to my patient and willing subjects, Christopher, Coco, and Zach Brooks, who fill my farm life with love.

About the Author

Amanda Brooks is the author of three books and a contributing editor and writer at *Condé Nast Traveler* and *Architectural Digest*. She has also written for *T: The New York Times Style Magazine, The Wall Street Journal, Vogue,* and British *Vogue*. The former fashion director of Barneys New York and creative director of Tuleh, Brooks has appeared as a fashion expert on *Today, The Early Show,* and NPR. She lives with her husband and their two children in Oxfordshire, England.

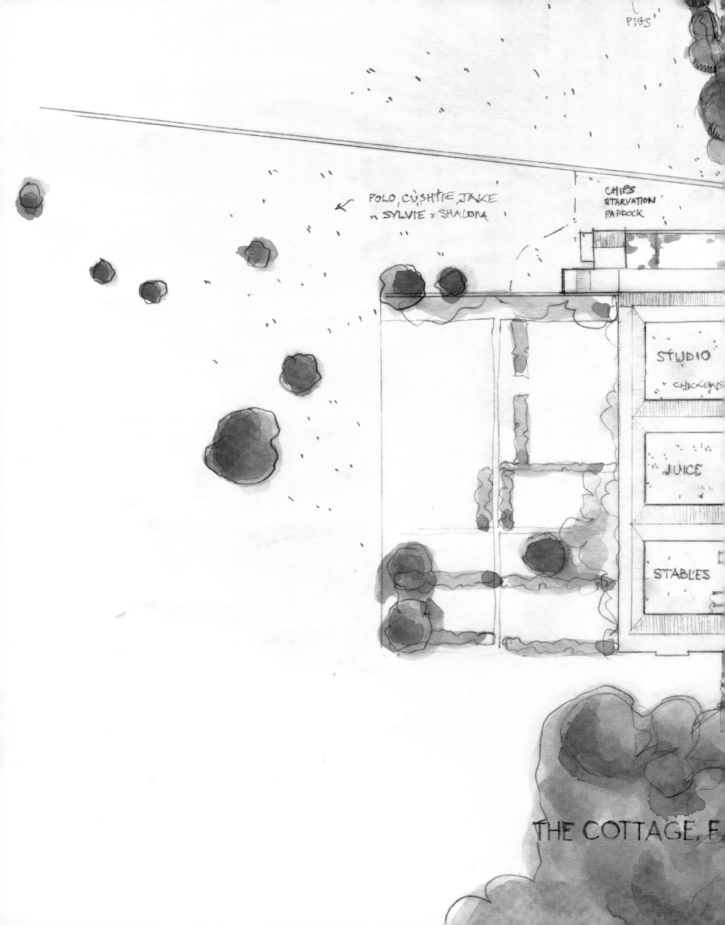

PIGS

POLO, CUSHTIE, JAKE
" SYLVIE & SHALONA "

CHIPS
STARVATION
PADROCK

STUDIO

CHICKENS

JUICE

STABLES

THE COTTAGE, F